STUDY GUIDE AND DEMONSTRATION PROBLEMS
CHAPTERS 16-27

PRINCIPLES OF FINANCIAL & MANAGEMENT ACCOUNTING

STUDY GUIDE AND DEMONSTRATION PROBLEMS
CHAPTERS 16-27

Judith Cassidy

PRINCIPLES OF FINANCIAL & MANAGEMENT ACCOUNTING

A CORPORATE APPROACH

Charles T. Horngren
Stanford University

Walter T. Harrison, Jr.
Baylor University

Michael A. Robinson
Baylor University

PRENTICE HALL, Englewood Cliffs, New Jersey 07632

A Paramount Communications Company
Englewood Cliffs, New Jersey 07632

Printed in the United States of America

10 9 8 7 6 5 4 3 2 1

ISBN 0-13-103425-1

Prentice-Hall International (UK) Limited, *London*
Prentice-Hall of Australia Pty. Limited, *Sydney*
Prentice-Hall Canada Inc., *Toronto*
Prentice-Hall Hispanoamericana, S.A., *Mexico*
Prentice-Hall of India Private Limited, *New Delhi*
Prentice-Hall of Japan, Inc., *Tokyo*
Simon & Schuster Asia Pte. Ltd., *Singapore*
Editora Prentice-Hall do Brasil, Ltda., *Rio de Janeiro*

Contents

To The Student

Study Guide, Chapters 16-27, is your aid to mastery of ***Principles of Financial and Management Accounting*** by Charles T. Horngren, Walter T. Harrison, and Michael A. Robinson. For each textbook chapter there is a corresponding *Study Guide* chapter containing three sections:

> ***1. Chapter Review.*** The chapter review is organized by the learning objectives of the text chapter. For each objective the review provides a brief discussion of principles, concepts, terms, and techniques.
>
> ***2. Test Yourself.*** The self-test contains matching, multiple choice, completion questions, and exercises. Fully explained answers are provided for immediate feedback. The self-tests help you in two ways. First, they pinpoint any weak spots so you know what to study harder. Second, they provide an efficient review for exams. All questions and exercises focus on the material that your instructors are mostly likely to test.
>
> ***3. Demonstration Problems.*** The demonstration problems combine all the major elements of the chapter. Working papers are included for your convenience in solving the problems. At the back of the book are complete solutions with step-by-step explanations. Many students purchase a separate booklet of demonstration problems. This *Study Guide* gives you a full set of demonstration problems, with working papers, at no additional cost.

In order to get the most out of you *Study Guide*, you must first pay careful attention to your instructor and to your text. As you read the text chapter assigned, ask yourself questions and make a note of anything you have trouble remembering or do not understand. Spend time on the exhibits. An understanding of the exhibits is crucial to learning the chapter. Work through the Summary Problems and all assignments. They will help you to understand the process of accounting. In addition:

> **Read the *Study Guide* chapter review.** This will reinforce the facts you need to remember and may help you find answers to some of your questions.
>
> **Test yourself.** Take the self-test and check your answers. Make notes of anything you have trouble remembering or do not understand.
>
> **Work the demonstration problem.** Then check the solution and follow the explanations. If you still have questions, take them to class.

Your *Study Guide* is a valuable tool to help you remember the facts and understand the process of accounting. Using it correctly will enhance your performance in class and on exams.

Judith Cassidy, University of Mississippi

ACKNOWLEDGMENTS

Thanks to John Gill of the University of Mississippi for reviewing both volumes of the *Study Guide* for accuracy. Thanks to Jim Emig of Villanova University and Betsy Willis of Baylor University for further checking for accuracy and correspondence to the second edition of the Horngren and Harrison *Accounting* text. Thanks also to the following professors who contributed to the accuracy of the *Study Guide*:

Allen B. Bess, University of Evansville

Virginia Brunell, Diablo Valley College

Carol Dilworth, University of Toronto

Richard L. Hodges, Western Michigan University

Greg A. Pratas, Texas Tech University

Vali Sorathia, Briar Cliff College

John Stone, Potomac State College

STUDY GUIDE AND DEMONSTRATION PROBLEMS
CHAPTERS 16-27

PRINCIPLES OF FINANCIAL & MANAGEMENT ACCOUNTING

16

Introduction To Management Accounting: The Master Budget

CHAPTER REVIEW

OBJECTIVE 1 - USE A PERFORMANCE REPORT.

Management accounting provides information to a company's managers to aid in planning for the future and controlling the operations of the company. Two important themes of management accounting are (1) the cost-benefit criterion and (2) behavioral implications. One valuable management tool is the *budget*. A budget is a financial plan for the future. It *provides direction* by allowing managers to set realistic goals for the future. It can act to *motivate employees* to meet the firm's goals if all levels of personnel are allowed a voice in preparing it. Since the budget is an overall company plan, it fosters *coordination between* departments. A budget can also be used to *evaluate performance* by comparing budgeted (planned) goals and actual results. The comparison of budgeted goals and actual results is often done by preparing a *performance report*. The performance report compares actual figures with budgeted figures in order to identify areas that need corrective action and serves as a guide for the next period's budget. A well designed budgeting system includes the *budget*, the *budget committee*, and the *budget period*. The budget committee (a group of individuals from inside the firm) oversees the preparation of the master budget.

OBJECTIVE 2 - BUDGET THE COMPONENTS OF THE INCOME STATEMENT.

The *master budget* has three components: (1) the operating budget, (2) the capital expenditures budget, and (3) the financial budget.

The *operating budget* starts with preparation of the sales or revenue budget, the purchases budget, the cost of goods sold budget, and the operating expense budget and culminates with the *budgeted income statement*. The budgeted income statement contains *budgeted amounts* rather than actual amounts.

You should study Exhibit 16-4 to understand the flow of information in preparation of the master budget.

Preparing the Budgeted Income Statement:

Step 1. Prepare the *sales budget* (Schedule A in your text). Remember that there is no way to accurately plan for inventory purchases or inventory levels without a sales budget. The sales budget will generally schedule sales for each month, and present a total for the entire budget period.

Step 2. Prepare a *schedule of the purchases*, *cost of goods sold*, and *inventory budgets* (Schedule B in your text). Remember that you need to buy enough to meet both expected sales levels and the desired ending inventory levels. If there is a beginning inventory, it reduces the amount of inventory you need to purchase.

PURCHASES = COST OF GOODS SOLD + ENDING INVENTORY - BEGINNING INVENTORY

Step 3. Calculate *budgeted operating expenses* (Schedule C in your text). Remember that some expenses vary with sales, such as sales commissions, while other expenses, such as rent, are fixed amounts from month to month.

OBJECTIVE 3 - PREPARE A BUDGETED INCOME STATEMENT.

The schedules prepared for the operating budget are now used to prepare the budgeted income statement. *Budgeted sales* on the income statement were determined by preparation of the sales budget. *Budgeted cost of goods sold* was determined by the preparation of the purchases, cost of goods sold, and inventory budgets. The *gross margin* is equal to sales minus cost of goods sold. *Operating expenses* were scheduled on the operating expense budget. *Operating income* is equal to the gross margin minus the operating expenses. The one remaining part of the budgeted income statement is *interest expense*, which is determined from the cash budget. Remember, all of these are *budgeted amounts*.

OBJECTIVE 4 - PREPARE A CASH BUDGET.

Budgeting cash collections from customers (Schedule D in your text) requires that you estimate (1) cash sales and (2) cash collections from credit sales. These amounts should be determined for each period contained in the budget. *Budgeted cash disbursements* are generally divided into budgeted cash disbursements for purchases (Schedule E) and budgeted cash disbursements for operating expenses (Schedule F).

The budgeted acquisition of long-term assets appears in the capital budget, which is discussed in more detail in Chapter 25.

Carefully study the statement of budgeted cash receipts and disbursements, Exhibit 16-6 in your text. To prepare a *cash budget*, perform these steps for each budget period:

(1) Add cash receipts from customers (Schedule D) to the beginning cash balance to determine cash available before financing.

(2) Calculate total cash disbursements. Subtract this total from the total you calculated in step (1) above. This equals the ending cash balance before financing.

(3) Subtract the minimum cash balance desired to obtain the cash excess or deficiency.

(4) If a cash deficiency exists, then borrowing will occur to cover the deficiency. If a cash excess exists and there was prior borrowing, there will be repayments of principal and interest expense applicable to the prior borrowing. Obtain the total effects of financing by adding cash borrowed or subtracting principal and interest payments.

(5) Calculate the ending cash balance: ending cash available before financing (from step (2) above) plus the total effects of financing (from step (4) above).

OBJECTIVE 6 - PREPARE A BUDGETED BALANCE SHEET.

The *budgeted balance sheet* is prepared using the budgeted income statement, cash budget, and schedules we have reviewed. The ending balance of some items, such as cash, is carried to the balance sheet directly from a budget or schedule. Other items, such as owners' equity, are carried from the previous balance sheet and adjusted for the activity specified in the budget. Study Exhibit 16-7 in your text.

Because the sales (or revenue) is the foundation of the master budget for all types of businesses, *sales forecasting* must be accurate and reliable.

OBJECTIVE 7 - USE A CONTINUOUS BUDGET.

A *continuous (or rolling) budget* covers a specific number of months and keeps adding a new month as the old month ends and is deleted. Using a continuous budget keeps the budget current and requires managers to plan ahead.

TEST YOURSELF

All the self-testing materials in this chapter focus on information and procedures that your instructor is likely to test in quizzes and examinations.

I. MATCHING - MATCH EACH NUMBERED TERM WITH ITS LETTERED DEFINITION.

____ 1. budget committee

____ 2. budget

____ 3. capital expenditures budget

____ 4. cash budget

____ 5. continuous budget

____ 6. financial budget

____ 7. master budget

____ 8. short-term, self-liquidating financing

____ 9. operating budget

A. A management tool for forecasting and planning a business's future

B. Budget that includes the major financial statements and supporting schedules

C. Group that oversees preparation of the master budget

D. Debt incurred to buy inventories; cash collections from the sale of inventory will be used to pay the debt

E. Details budgeted cash receipts and disbursements for a period of time

F. Plan for purchases of property, plant, and equipment and other assets that management uses to produce revenues over a long period of time

G. Projects the means of raising money from stockholders and creditors and plans for cash management

H. Sets the target revenues and expenses - and thus net income - for the period

I. Systematically adds a month or a quarter as the month or quarter just ended is deleted

II. MULTIPLE CHOICE - CIRCLE THE CORRECT ANSWER.

1. A good budgeting system includes all of the following *except:*

   A. overly optimistic budget figures
   B. the budget committee
   C. the budget period
   D. the budget

2. Which of the following is *not* an advantage of the budgeting process?

   A. coordinates activities
   B. helps performance evaluation
   C. hinders management performance
   D. motivates employees

3. Which of the following is an *adverse* consequence of ending a period with too much inventory?

   A. gaining a customer who needs the goods immediately
   B. increased costs of carrying inventory
   C. decreased costs of carrying inventory
   D. inability to deliver goods when customers need them

4. Which of the following equations is proper for a retail company?

   A. beginning inventory + cost of goods sold + ending inventory = purchases
   B. beginning inventory + cost of goods sold - ending inventory = purchases
   C. ending inventory + purchases - beginning inventory = cost of goods sold
   D. beginning inventory + purchases - ending inventory = cost of goods sold

5. Which of the following equations is *not* correct relating to a cash budget?

   A. cash receipts - cash disbursements - beginning cash = ending cash
   B. beginning cash - cash disbursements + cash receipts = ending cash
   C. beginning cash + cash receipts - ending cash = cash disbursements
   D. ending cash + cash disbursements - cash receipts = beginning cash

6. Managers set:

   A. short-range goals
   B. long-range goals
   C. both short-range goals and long-range goals
   D. managers do not set goals

7. The last item computed for the budgeted income statement is:

   A. sales
   B. cost of goods sold
   C. capital expenditures
   D. interest expense

III. COMPLETION - COMPLETE EACH OF THE FOLLOWING STATEMENTS.

1. Accounting designed to report to parties inside the business is called

   ____ accounting.

2. The master budget includes the following budgets:

   ______________________________ ______________________________

   ____

3. The ____________________ budget plans cash management and projects the means of raising money from stockholders and creditors.

4. The ____________________ budget sets target revenues and expenses for the period.

5. The ____________________ is the starting point for the master budget.

6. Sales commissions and delivery expenses typically increase as

____ increase.

7. A ____________________________ budget systematically adds a month or quarter as the month or quarter just ended is deleted.

IV. EXERCISES

1. Zz Sleep Shop's cash budget for the first three quarters of 19X9 is given below (note that some of the data is missing and must be calculated). Zz requires a minimum cash balance of at least $20,000, and owes $2,000 on a note payable from a previous quarter. (Ignore interest.)

Zz Sleep Shop
Quarterly Cash Budget
19X9

	1	2	3
Beginning cash balance	$ 32,000	$ D	$ 26,000
Add collections from customers	A	140,000	134,000
Cash available	$ B	$ E	$160,000
Deduct disbursements			
Inventory purchases	$ 62,000	$ F	$ 46,000
Operating expenses	50,000	44,000	60,000
Equipment purchases	20,000	22,000	58,000
Dividends	0	12,000	J
Total disbursements	$132,000	$ G	$ K
Excess (deficiency) in cash	$ 14,000	$ 34,000	($ 4,000)
Financing			
Add borrowing	C	-	$ 24,000
Deduct repayments	-	H	0
Ending cash balance	$ 20,000	$ I	$ 20,000

Required: Find the missing value represented by each letter. (Hint - it may not be possible to solve this problem in sequence, A first, B second, and so on.)

A.

B.

C.

D.

E.

F.

G.

H.

I.

J.

K.

2. If Inventory increased by $1,000 during the year and Cost of Goods Sold was $40,000, what was Purchases?

3. If ending Cash is twice the amount of beginning Cash, Cash receipts are $150,000, and Cash disbursements are two-thirds of Cash receipts, determine beginning and ending Cash balances.

4. Budgeted sales of tree ornaments were 80,000 for December. It takes 5 yards of ribbon to make one ornament. Actual and budgeted inventories are as follows on December 1 and 31.

	Dec. 1 (Actual)	Dec. 31 (Budgeted)
Ornaments	20,000	100
Ribbon	40,000 yards	250 yards

A. How many ornaments must be produced in December?

B. How many yards of ribbon must be purchased in December?

SOLUTIONS

I. MATCHING

1. C   2. A   3. F   4. E   5. I   6. G   7. B   8. D   9. H

II. MULTIPLE CHOICE

1. A — Of the items listed, B, C, and D are all part of a good budgeting system. By now in this course you should intuitively recognize that such things as "overly optimistic" budget figures have no place in accounting.

2. C — The budget process does not hinder management performance, it enhances it. Answers A, B, and C are all advantages of the budgeting process.

3. B — Answer A is one of the few positive consequences of carrying too much inventory. As to answer C, it is doubtful that carrying too much inventory will decrease costs. Answer D makes no sense.

4. D — Purchases = Desired ending inventory + cost of goods sold - beginning inventory.

5. A — The correct formula for answer A would require the addition of beginning cash instead of its subtraction.

6. C — Both short and long-range goal setting are important parts of every manager's job.

7. D — Interest expense comes from the cash budget and requires that all other budgets be completed and all other calculations for the income statement be complete.

III. COMPLETION

1. management
2. operating budget, capital expenditures budget, financial budget
3. financial
4. operating
5. sales forecast
6. sales
7. continuous or rolling

IV. EXERCISES

1. Solution is given in the order in which the exercise may be worked.

B. Cash available - Total disbursements = Excess (deficiency)

B - $132,000 = $14,000

B = $146,000

A. Beginning cash balance + Cash collections = Cash available

$32,000 + A = $146,000

A = $114,000

C. Excess + Borrowing = Ending cash balance

$14,000 + C = $20,000

C = $6,000

D. $20,000; the beginning cash balance for any quarter is the ending cash balance from the previous quarter.

E. Beginning cash balance + Cash collections = Cash available

$20,000 + $140,000 = E

E = $160,000

I. $26,000; the ending cash balance for any quarter is the beginning cash balance for the next quarter.

H. Excess - Repayments = Ending cash balance

$34,000 - H = $26,000

H = $8,000

G. Cash available - Total disbursements = Excess

$160,000 - G = $34,000

G = $126,000

F. Inventory purchases + Operating expenses + Equipment purchases + dividends = Total disbursements

F + $44,000 + $22,000 + $12,000 = $126,000

F = $48,000

K. Cash available - Total disbursements = (deficiency)

$160,000 - L = ($4,000)

$160,000 + $4,000 = L

$164,000 = L

J. (Inventory purchases + Operating expenses + Equipment purchases) + dividends = Total disbursements

($46,000 + $60,000 + $58,000) + K = $164,000

$164,000 + K = $164,000

K = $ -0-

2. Beginning Inventory + Purchases - Ending Inventory = Cost of Goods Sold

X + Purchases - (X + $1,000) = $40,000
X + Purchases - X - $1,000 = $40,000
Purchases = $41,000

3. Beginning Cash = X
Ending Cash = 2 X
Cash disbursements = 2/3 X $150,000 = $100,000

Beg. Cash + Cash Rec. - Cash Disb. = End. Cash
X + $150,000 - $100,000 = 2 X
Beginning Cash = X = $50,000
Ending Cash = 2 X = $100,000

4. A. Sales + End. Inv. - Beg. Inv. = Ornaments Produced
80,000 + 100 - 20,000 = 60,100

B. Production + End. Inv. - Beg. Inv. = Ribbon Purchases in Yds
(60,100 X 5) + 250 - 40,000 = 260,750

DEMONSTRATION PROBLEM

McGregor's Seeds
Balance Sheet
June 30, 19X9

ASSETS		LIABILITIES	
Cash	$ 5,000	Accounts payable	$ 11,000
Accounts receivable	10,800		
Inventory	12,000	OWNER'S EQUITY	
Building and equipment (net)	90,000	McGregor, capital	106,800
Total Assets	$117,800	Total liabilities and owner's equity	$117,800

Sales in June were $30,000. Sales for the next four months are estimated to be $50,000 for July, $70,000 for August, $30,000 for September, and $25,000 for October. Each unit of inventory sells for $5. Ten percent of each month's sales are for cash. The remaining sales on account are collected 60% in the month of the sale and 40% in the month following the sale. McGregor's salespersons are paid a commission of 5% of sales. Commissions are paid in the month of the sale.

Purchases for June were $20,000. Each unit of inventory costs $2. Purchases are paid for 70% in the month of purchase and 30% in the month following purchase. McGregor wishes to have inventory on hand at the end of each month equal to 60% of cost of goods sold for the following month.

The business purchased a delivery truck in August for $25,750 in cash.

The business has a policy of maintaining a minimum cash balance of $4,000. McGregor's line of credit at the bank requires borrowing and repayment of principal in increments of $1,000. The interest rate on this line of credit is 1% per month with borrowing taking place at the beginning of the month and repayments at the end of the month.

Depreciation for July and August is $4,000. Depreciation for September is $4,700. Insurance expense of $3,000 is paid monthly. Other operating expenses are expected to be $12,000 in July, $22,000 in August, and $18,000 in September. Other operating expenses are paid 50% in the month incurred and 50% in the following month.

REQUIRED:
1. Prepare a sales budget for the next quarter.
2. Prepare a purchases, cost of goods sold, and inventory budget for the next quarter.
3. Prepare an operating expense budget for the next quarter.
4. Prepare a budget for cash disbursements for purchases.
5. Prepare a budget for cash disbursements for operating expenses.
6. Prepare a schedule of cash collections.
7. Prepare a cash budget.
8. Prepare a budgeted income statement for the quarter.
9. Prepare a budgeted balance sheet for September 30, 19X9.

NOTE TO STUDENT:
SOLUTIONS TO DEMONSTRATION PROBLEMS APPEAR AT THE END OF THIS VOLUME.

Requirement 1

Sales Budget

	July	August	September	Total

Requirement 2

Purchases, Cost of Goods Sold, and Inventory Budget

	July	August	September	Total

Requirement 3

Operating Expenses Budget

	July	August	September	Total

Requirement 4

Budgeted Cash Disbursements for Purchases

	July	August	September

Requirement 5

Budgeted Cash Disbursements for Operating Expenses

	July	August	September

Requirement 6

Schedule of Cash Collections

	July	August	September	Total

Space for requirements 7 and 8 is on the following pages.

Requirement 9

McGregor's Seeds
Budgeted Balance Sheet
September 30, 19X9

ASSETS		LIABILITIES	

Requirement 7

Cash Budget

	July	August	September

Requirement 8

McGregor's Seeds
Budgeted Income Statement
For the Quarter Ended September 30, 19X9

17

Cost-Volume-Profit Relationships And The Contribution Margin Approach To Decision Making

CHAPTER REVIEW

OBJECTIVE 1 - IDENTIFY DIFFERENT COST BEHAVIOR PATTERNS.

Cost behavior is the way that costs change in response to changes in business activity. A *cost driver* is any factor that can cause a change in the costs related to it. The three patterns of cost behavior are variable, fixed, and mixed.

Total variable costs change in direct proportion to changes in volume or level of activity. Examples of variable costs include cost of goods sold, sales commissions, and delivery expense. Suppose VCR tapes have a cost of $4 per tape when purchased for resale. If a retailer sells 1,000 tapes, cost of goods sold will be $4,000. However, if 2,000 tapes are sold, cost of goods sold will be $8,000. Thus, the more tapes the retailer sells, the higher the cost of goods sold will be since the $4 variable cost/unit is constant.

Total fixed costs do not change as volume changes. Examples of fixed costs include expenses such as rent and depreciation. Suppose the rent for a store is $5,000 per month. The store owner will pay $5,000 per month whether sales increase, decrease, or remain the same.

Mixed costs (also called semivariable costs) are part variable and part fixed. The monthly telephone bill, for example, is based both on local service and long distance service. The amount for local (unlimited) service is a fixed cost, while the amount for long distance service is a variable cost. Therefore, the total telephone bill is a mixed cost.

Study the graphs in your text which illustrate cost behavior patterns (Exhibits 17-1, 17-2, and 17-3). The variable cost graph begins at the origin (zero volume, zero cost). Variable cost increases in a straight line, whose slope equals the variable cost per unit. The slope of the line gets steeper the more the variable cost per unit increases. The fixed cost graph is a horizontal line that intersects the cost (vertical) axis at the fixed cost level. The mixed cost graph intersects the cost axis at the level of the fixed cost component, and its slope equals the variable cost per unit.

When budgeting costs, companies use the *relevant range* concept. Relevant range is the predictable band of activity or volume of operations.

OBJECTIVE 2 - USE A CONTRIBUTION MARGIN INCOME STATEMENT TO MAKE BUSINESS DECISIONS.

The *conventional income statement* focuses on the perspective of external users of financial statements. It has the format:

	Sales
-	Cost of Goods Sold
=	Gross Margin
-	Operating Expenses
=	Income from Operations

Note that the conventional income statement classifies expenses according to their *function,* such as cost of goods sold or operating expenses.

The contribution margin income statement focuses on the contribution margin, the excess of sales over variable expenses. It classifies expenses according to cost behavior, which will be either variable or fixed. It has the format:

	Sales
-	Variable Expenses
=	Contribution Margin
-	Fixed Expenses
=	Income from Operations

The contribution margin income statement is a useful management tool. Once fixed expenses are covered, the balance of the contribution margin "contributes" to income. Since fixed expenses remain constant, when the contribution margin changes, income will change by the same amount. Remember that, in general, variable expenses will change proportionately with sales. Thus, if sales increase by 10 percent, variable expenses will increase by 10 percent, and the contribution margin will increase by 10 percent.

Using the contribution margin income statement, it is possible to calculate exactly how a change in sales will affect profit. Similar analysis using the conventional income statement is not possible.

OBJECTIVE 3 - COMPUTE BREAK-EVEN SALES.

Cost-volume-profit analysis is often called *break-even analysis*. The break-even point is the point at which total revenue equals total expenses. At the break-even point, profit is zero. If sales are below the break-even point, the result is a loss. If sales are above the break-even point, the result is a profit.

Decision makers use cost-volume-profit analysis to answer questions such as, "How much do we need to sell to break even?" or "If our sales are some specific amount, what will our profit be?"

Two approaches used in cost-volume-profit (or CVP) analysis are the *equation approach* and the *contribution margin approach*. With either approach, start by separating total expenses into variable expenses and fixed expenses.

The equation approach is:

Sales - Variable Expenses = Fixed Expenses + Operating Income

Operating income is zero at break-even. The equation shows how many units must be sold (and the total dollar amount of the sales) in order to break even.

The contribution margin approach is:

$$\text{Contribution Margin} = \text{Sales} - \text{Variable Costs}$$

The contribution margin receives its name because it contributes to the payment of fixed costs and operating income.

The contribution margin may be expressed on a per-unit basis, or as a percentage or ratio:

$$\text{Contribution Margin Per Unit} = \text{Sales Price Per Unit} - \text{Variable Expense Per Unit}$$

$$\text{Contribution Margin Percentage or Ratio} = \frac{\text{Contribution Margin}}{\text{Selling Price}}$$

Break-even sales in units is computed by dividing fixed expenses by the contribution margin per unit:

$$\text{Break-Even Sales in Units} = \frac{\text{Fixed Expenses}}{\text{Contribution Margin Per Unit}}$$

Break-even sales in dollars is computed by dividing fixed expenses by the contribution margin percentage:

$$\text{Break-Even Sales in Dollars} = \frac{\text{Fixed Expenses}}{\text{Contribution Margin Percentage}}$$

Review the examples in the text (Questions 1-4) so that you know what will happen to the break-even point if a fixed cost is changed, if the sale price is changed, or if the variable cost per unit is changed. If fixed costs or variable costs increase, break-even increases. If the sale price increases, break-even decreases.

OBJECTIVE 4 - COMPUTE THE SALES LEVEL NEEDED TO EARN A TARGET OPERATING INCOME.

The profit that a business wishes to earn is called the *target operating income*.

$$\text{Target Sales in Units} = \frac{\text{Fixed Expenses} + \text{Target Operating Income}}{\text{Contribution Margin Per Unit}}$$

$$\text{Target Sales in Dollars} = \frac{\text{Fixed Expenses} + \text{Target Operating Income}}{\text{Contribution Margin Percentage}}$$

Notice that the only difference between computing break-even sales and target sales is that with target sales, the target operating income amount is added to fixed expenses.

OBJECTIVE 5 - GRAPH A SET OF COST-VOLUME-PROFIT RELATIONSHIPS.

Often, a business is interested in knowing the amount of operating income or operating loss to expect at various levels of sales. One convenient way to provide this information is to prepare a *cost-volume-profit graph*.

In order to familiarize yourself with components of the CVP graph, cover the answers below and practice labeling the graph.

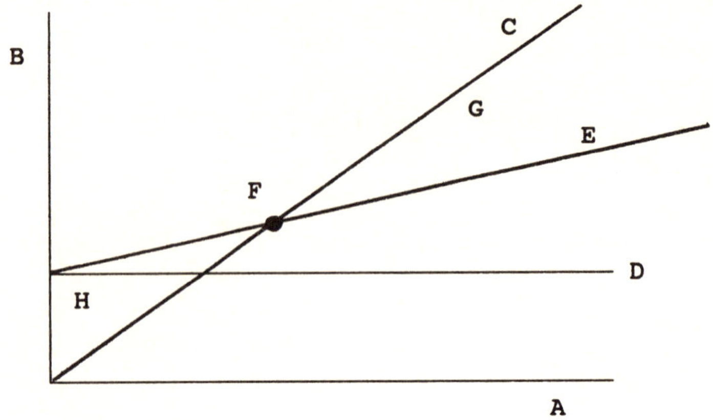

The correct answers are:

A.	Units	E.	Total expense (Cost) line
B.	Dollars	F.	Break-even sales point
C.	Sales line (Total Revenue)	G.	Operating income area
D.	Fixed expense line	H.	Operating loss area

OBJECTIVE 6 - COMPUTE A MARGIN OF SAFETY.

The *margin of safety* is the excess of expected or actual sales over break-even sales. It tells a business how much sales can drop before an operating loss is incurred. The margin of safety may be computed in terms of either dollars or units:

Margin of Safety = Expected Sales - Break-Even Sales

Sales Mix

One of the basic assumptions underlying CVP analysis is that the *sales mix,* the combination of products that make up total sales, does not change.

Break-even problems involving multiple products can be solved using either the contribution margin approach or the equation approach. The contribution approach is illustrated in your text. The equation approach to the *same problem* is given below:

Since 5 large posters are sold for every 4 regular posters, let

5 X = the number of large posters sold

and

4 X = the number of regular posters sold

Then:

Σ (Sales - Variable Expenses) = Fixed Expenses

4 X * $1.40 + 5 X * $2.08 = $700

X = 43.75 units

Breakeven sales for large posters = 5 * 43.75 = 175 units

Breakeven sales for regular posters = 4 * 43.75 = 219 units*

* Note that fractions of a unit should always be rounded *upward*.

TEST YOURSELF

All the self-testing materials in this chapter focus on information and procedures that your instructor is likely to test in quizzes and examinations.

I. MATCHING - MATCH EACH NUMBERED TERM WITH ITS LETTERED DEFINITION.

____ 1. cost behavior

____ 2. variable cost

____ 3. fixed cost

____ 4. mixed cost

____ 5. break-even point

____ 6. contribution margin

____ 7. target operating income

____ 8. margin of safety

____ 9. relevant range

____10. high-low method

A. The amount of unit sales or dollar sales at which revenue equals expenses

B. A way to separate mixed expenses into variable and fixed expenses

C. The description of how costs change in response to a shift in the volume of business activity

D. The excess of sale price over variable expenses

E. A band of activity or volume in which actual operations are likely to occur

F. A cost that does not change in total as volume changes

G. The excess of expected (or actual) sales over break-even sales

H. A cost that is part variable and part fixed

I. A cost that changes in total in direct proportion to changes in volume or activity

J. The desired income a business wishes to earn

II. MULTIPLE CHOICE - CIRCLE THE CORRECT ANSWER.

Use the following information for Questions 1 through 4:

Angelo Co. sells floppy diskettes. Last year Angelo sold 5,500 boxes at $12 per box. The variable cost per box was $7.20 and fixed costs amounted to $14,400.

1. The break-even point in boxes of floppy diskettes was:

   A. 1,200
   B. 2,000
   C. 3,000
   D. 5,500

2. The break-even point in sales dollars was:

   A. $66,000
   B. $36,000
   C. $24,000
   D. $14,400

3. The margin of safety in dollars was:

A. $30,000
B. $48,000
C. $51,000
D. $ -0-

4. If Angelo wished to earn an operating income of $17,400, how many boxes of floppy diskettes would have to be sold?

A. 3,600
B. 4,400
C. 5,500
D. 6,625

5. Dividing break-even sales dollars by the unit selling price results in the:

A. Variable cost per unit
B. Break-even point in dollars
C. Break-even point in units
D. Variable cost ratio

6. Which of the following will *decrease* the break-even point?

A. Decreasing fixed costs
B. Increasing fixed costs
C. Increasing variable cost per unit
D. Decreasing selling price

7. Which of the following will *increase* the break-even point?

A. Decreasing fixed costs
B. Increasing selling price
C. Decreasing variable cost per unit
D. Decreasing selling price

III. COMPLETION - COMPLETE EACH OF THE FOLLOWING STATEMENTS.

1. The ______________________________ is equal to the selling price per unit minus the variable expenses per unit.

2. A convenient way to determine operating income or loss at various levels of sales is to prepare a ______________________________.

3. ________________________ and ___________________________ are examples of costs that change proportionally with sales.

4. ______________________________ is a way to separate a mixed cost into its fixed and variable components.

5. Two approaches used in CVP analysis are the ____________________________ approach and the ____ approach.

6. ________________________________ tells a decision maker how much sales can drop before an operating loss is incurred.

For each of the following, complete the sentence with **increase**, **decrease**, or **not affect**.

7. An increase in direct material cost will __________________________ the contribution margin.

8. An increase in direct labor cost will ______________________________ the break-even point.

9. A decrease in direct materials cost will __________________________ the break-even point.

10. An increase in fixed plant insurance will ____________________ the break-even point.

11. A decrease in fixed advertising expense will ____________________ the break-even point.

12. A decrease in fixed advertising expense will ____________________ the contribution margin.

IV. EXERCISES

1. Carpet World's fixed costs are $640,000. Variable costs are 20% of sales. What is the break-even point in sales dollars?

2. Winchell's fixed costs are $27,000. Variable costs are $3 per unit. How many units must Winchell sell at $5 to break even?

3. Creole Company has a break-even point of 70,000 units. The selling price is $6.25 per unit and variable costs are $3.80 per unit. What are Creole's fixed costs?

4. Cinnamon Sticks sells boxes of ground cinnamon and packages of cinnamon sticks. Boxes sell for $2.50 and packages sell for $3.50. Variable costs are $1.25 for boxes and $2.75 for packages. Sticks expects to sell 2,000 boxes of ground cinnamon and 500 packages of sticks. Fixed costs are $1610. What is the break-even point?

SOLUTIONS

I. MATCHING

1. C 2. I 3. F 4. H 5. A 6. D 7. J 8. G 9. E 10. B

II. MULTIPLE CHOICE

1. C $14,400 / ($12.00 - $7.20) = 3,000

2. B $14,400 / [($12.00 - $7.20)/$12.00] = $36,000

3. A (5,500 boxes - 3,000 boxes) X $12.00 = $30,000

4. D ($14,400 + $17,400) / [($12.00 - $7.20)/$12.00] = 6,625

5. C BE$ = Break-even sales dollars. BEu = Break-even in units.

   $Pu = unit selling price.

   BE$ = BEu X $Pu

   BE$/$Pu = BEu

6. A BE$ = Break-even sales dollars. BEu = Break-even in units.

   $Pu = unit selling price. FC = Fixed Cost.
   VCu = Variable cost per unit.

   Recall that BEu = FC /($Pu - VCu)

   Of the Answers listed, only A "Decreasing fixed costs" will decrease the break-even point.

7. D Refer to 6 above. Note that answer D, "Decreasing selling price," will decrease the contribution margin and increase the break-even point.

   Note: If you had difficulty with 5 through 7, consider the formula for the break-even point in units:

$$\frac{\text{Fixed Expenses}}{\text{Contribution Margin Per Unit}} = \text{Break-Even in Units}$$

   If the numerator increases, or the denominator decreases, the break-even point increases. If the numerator decreases, or the denominator increases, the break-even point decreases.

III. COMPLETION

1. contribution margin per unit
2. cost-volume-profit graph
3. Cost of goods sold, selling commission (other answers may be acceptable)
4. The high-low
5. equation, contribution margin
6. The margin of safety
7. decrease
   (An increase in direct materials is an increase in the variable cost per unit. This decreases the contribution margin.)
8. increase
   (An increase in direct labor cost is an increase in the variable cost per unit. This decreases the contribution margin. As the contribution margin decreases, the break-even point increases.)
9. decrease
   (A decrease in direct materials cost is a decrease in variable cost per unit. This increases the contribution margin. As the contribution margin increases, the break-even point decreases. Contrast with #8.)
10. increase
    (An increase in plant insurance is an increase in fixed costs. An increase in fixed costs increases the break-even point.)
11. decrease
    (A decrease in fixed advertising expense is a decrease in fixed costs. Therefore the break-even point decreases. Contrast with #10.)
12. not affect
    (A decrease in fixed advertising expense is a decrease in fixed costs. Changes in fixed costs have no effect on the contribution margin.)

IV. EXERCISES

1. If VC are 20% of sales, then the CM% is 80%, (1 - 20%)

$$\frac{\text{Fixed Expenses}}{\text{Contribution Margin Ratio}} = \text{Break-Even in Dollars}$$

$$\frac{\$640{,}000}{80\%} = \$800{,}000$$

2.

$$\frac{\text{Fixed Expenses}}{\text{Contribution Margin Per Unit}} = \text{Break-Even in Units}$$

$$\frac{\$27{,}000}{\$5 - \$3} = 13{,}500$$

3.

$$\frac{\text{Fixed Expenses}}{\text{Contribution Margin Per Unit}} = \text{Break-Even in Units}$$

$$\frac{FE}{\$6.25 - \$3.80} = 70{,}000$$

$$FE = \$171{,}500$$

4.

	Boxes Ground Cinnamon		Packages Cinnamon Sticks	Total
Sales price per unit	$2.50		$3.50	
Variable expense per unit	1.25		2.75	
Contribution Margin per unit	$1.25		$ .75	
Estimated Sales in units	X 2,000		X 500	2,500
Estimated Contribution Margin	$2,500	+	$375	= $2,875
Weighted-average contribution margin per unit ($2,875/2,500)				$ 1.15

$$\text{Break-even sales in units} = \frac{\text{Fixed expenses}}{\text{Weighted-average Contribution Margin}} = \frac{\$1,610}{\$1.15} =$$

$$\text{Break-even sales of boxes of ground cinnamon} = \frac{1,400 \text{ X } 2,000}{2,500} = \underline{\underline{1,120}} \text{ boxes}$$

$$\text{Break-even sales of packages of cinnamon sticks} = \frac{1,400 \text{ X } 500}{2,500} = \underline{\underline{280}} \text{ packages}$$

DEMONSTRATION PROBLEM

Part A

Outer Space Toy Company plans to market its newest toy, a miniature robot, for a selling price of $40. Sales are expected to be between 15,000 and 45,000 robots during 19X9. Outer Space will incur a total of $760,000 in expenses to sell 15,000 robots and a total of $1,480,000 in expenses to sell 45,000 robots.

REQUIRED:

1. Use the contribution margin approach to compute Outer Space's break-even sales in units and in dollars.

2. How many robots must Outer Space sell to earn an operating income of $80,000?

3. Suppose Outer Space increases the sale price to $48 per robot. How many robots must Outer Space sell to earn an operating income of $80,000?

4. Prepare a graph showing operating income and operating loss areas from 0 to 50,000 robots, assuming that the original selling price of $40 is in effect. Mark the break-even sales level and the sales level needed to earn an operating income of $80,000.

Part B

During 19X9, Outer Space sold 35,000 robots at $40 each. Cost of goods sold equals 55% of variable expenses, while operating expenses equal 45% of variable expenses. All of the fixed expenses, which were calculated in Part A, are operating expenses.

REQUIRED:

1. Prepare a contribution margin income statement for the year 19X9.

Part A

Requirement 1 (break-even sales in units and dollars)

Requirement 2 (target operating income)

Requirement 3 (effect of change in selling price)

Requirement 4 (graph)

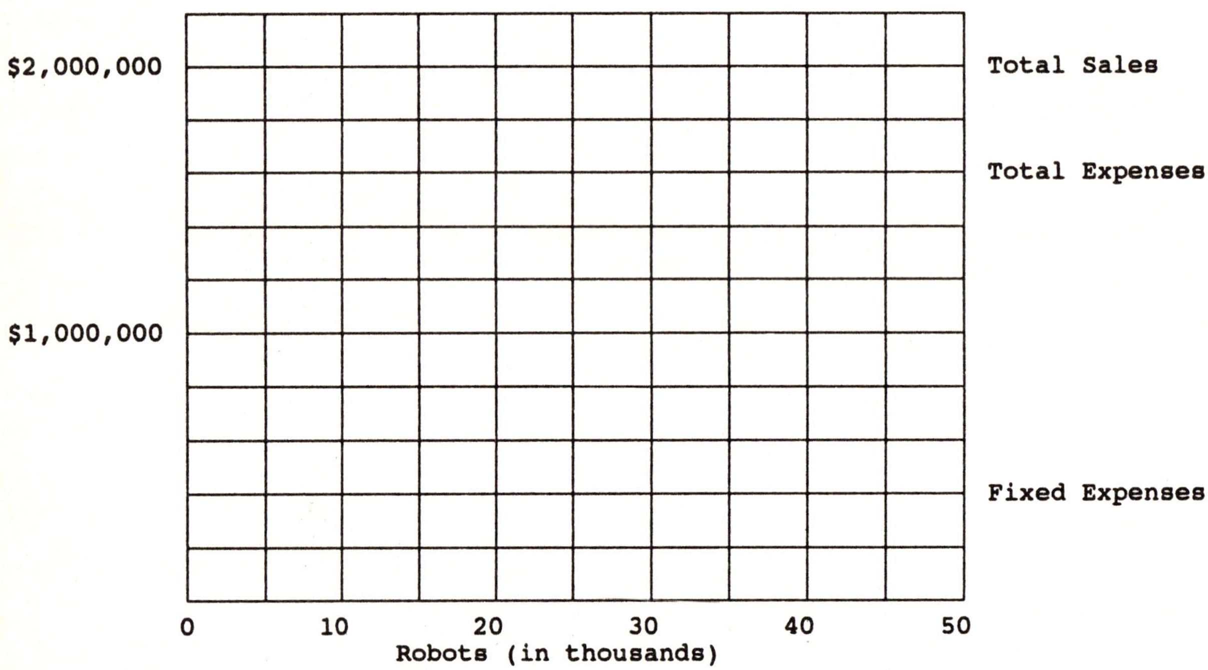

18

Cost Behavior Analysis

CHAPTER REVIEW

OBJECTIVE 1 - IDENTIFY TYPES OF FIXED COSTS.

Fixed costs are ordinarily categorized as either committed fixed costs or discretionary fixed costs.

Committed fixed costs typically occur because a company owns or controls property, plant, and equipment (inputs). Examples of committed fixed costs include depreciation, property taxes, and amounts related to long-term leases. These costs are extremely difficult to change in the short run. The amounts are fixed regardless of the level of production (outputs).

OBJECTIVE 2 - USE COST BEHAVIOR ANALYSIS TO MAKE BUSINESS DECISIONS.

Managers set goals and make decisions. One goal is to maximize operating income over a period of time. To achieve this objective, managers must attempt to match the company's capacity to provide goods and services to the expected demand for those goods and services. Why? First, capacity costs money. Remember that committed fixed costs, such as depreciation on a factory building, occur whether one unit or one million units of product are produced. Second, a company must have the capacity to meet demand. A company cannot sell two million units of product if it can only produce one million units of product. Without adequate capacity, a company may lose profitable sales.

One way to make this analysis is to (1) identify the possible alternatives, and (2) examine changes in the contribution margin and fixed expenses. Study Exhibit 18-2 in your text carefully. In this exhibit, the alternatives are a smaller store or a larger store. The larger store has higher fixed expenses, but also has the capacity for greater sales volume.

In addition, managers often analyze the effects of differences in demand. Exhibit 18-3 in your text reflects such an analysis.

OBJECTIVE 3 - IDENTIFY TWO APPROACHES FOR CONTROLLING OPERATING LABOR COSTS.

Discretionary fixed costs result from top-management decisions and policies. These decisions normally are reflected in periodic budgets and lack a clear relationship between inputs and outputs. These costs might include fixed advertising and public relations costs, training programs, research, and management salaries. A company can choose to reduce the amount of discretionary fixed costs in difficult circumstances. For example, a company may temporarily reduce a discretionary fixed cost such as research expenditures. However, a company cannot temporarily reduce a committed fixed cost such as the depreciation expense associated with a factory.

Variable costs may also be classified. Two categories of variable costs are engineered variable costs and discretionary variable costs. Engineered variable costs are usually related to production and distribution and can be measured and observed. For example, the time it takes a worker to sew a garment can be measured and observed. Discretionary variable costs usually result from management decisions. For example, management may decide to base the advertising budget on sales, either as a percentage of sales or as an amount per unit of product sold. In this example, advertising is now a variable cost instead of a fixed cost. It is discretionary because management can change the method of computing the advertising budget, and because it is difficult to identify a clear cause-and-effect relationship between advertising and sales.

The discretionary-fixed-cost approach to manage labor costs relies primarily on personal supervision to control labor costs. Managers can observe the work activity in a department, and may also analyze the quantity of output generated by workers.

The engineered-variable-cost approach develops a budget formula to help determine the number of employees needed. The formula is a function of salary and output.

Refer to Exhibit 18-5 in your text for a graphic comparison of the two approaches.

OBJECTIVE 4 - COMPUTE THE EQUAL-COST VOLUME OF TWO COST BEHAVIOR PATTERNS.

Companies often have choices about how to incur costs. Trade-offs arise between variable costs and fixed costs. One example is whether to pay salespeople a (discretionary fixed) salary plus a (variable) commission, or whether to pay only commission.

To determine which payment plan is preferable, you must compute the sales level at which the costs of both plans are equal. This sales level is the point of indifference. The plan you choose will depend on whether you expect sales to be greater than or less than the point of indifference.

OBJECTIVE 5 - GRAPH THE THREE MAJOR TYPES OF COST FUNCTIONS.

Cost functions are based on two major assumptions. First, cost behavior can be explained by one cost driver. Second, the cost function is linear over the relevant range. Some non-linear functions, such as the step-function variable cost (Exhibit 18-7), may also be represented in a linear form without a great degree of error.

The basic cost function takes the form:

$$y = a + bx$$

In this equation, y represents total cost, a represents fixed cost, b represents variable cost per unit, and x represents the number of units.

The three major cost functions are variable, fixed, and mixed. A mixed cost includes both fixed and variable components. Refer to Exhibit 18-8 for a graphical representation of these cost functions.

OBJECTIVE 6 - USE THREE METHODS TO ESTIMATE MIXED-COST FUNCTIONS.

Estimating a mixed-cost function requires four steps. First, you must choose a cost driver. A cost driver is some activity which can be used to explain what causes the cost to occur. Examples of cost drivers are in Exhibit 18-9 in your text. The second step is to collect a sample of data on the cost and the cost driver. Step three is to plot the data on a graph. Finally, the fourth step is to estimate the cost function.

Three methods used to estimate mixed-cost functions are (1) the high-low method, (2) the visual-fit method, and (3) the least-squares regression method.

The high-low method estimates a cost function using only the highest and lowest volume points and the related total costs from a sample of data. On a graph, you would plot the data points, and connect the highest and lowest volume data points with a straight line. The intercept represents the fixed portion of total cost. Refer to Exhibit 18-13, Panel A.

We can also use a mathematical approach to the high-low method. The first step is to find the high and low volume points and their related total costs in the data sample. These points are levels of cost driver activity such as labor hours or machine hours, and are represented in the cost function by the variable x. The associated total costs are represented in the cost function as variable y.

The next step is to find the variable rate per unit of volume. In the cost function, the variable rate is expressed as variable b. The equation to find the variable rate is:

$$\text{Variable rate} = \frac{\text{Change in costs}}{\text{Change in volume}}$$

The change in costs is the difference between the costs associated with the high and low volume points. The change in volume is the difference between the high volume point and the low volume point.

The third step is to find the fixed cost component a. We can mathematically rearrange the equation $y = a + bx$ as $a = y - bx$. Since b is the variable rate, and x is the volume, bx is the total variable component of the total cost, and we can express the equation as:

$$\text{Fixed component} = \text{Total mixed cost} - \text{variable component}$$

Because the variable component b is a function of both the high and low volumes, you may calculate the fixed component a by using <u>either</u> the high or low volume observation.

The visual-fit method is the simplest to use. After plotting your data points on a graph, you attempt to draw a straight line on the graph, coming close to as many of the data points as you can. You should find that about half the data points are above the line and half are below the line. Then, draw a horizontal line from the intercept point parallel to the x-axis. Draw a vertical line parallel to the y-axis near any of the data points. Find the values of x and y at the intersection of these two lines, and substitute the values of x, y, and the fixed cost intercept a into the equation $y = a + bx$. Refer to Exhibit 18-13, Panel B.

Least-squares regression is usually performed using computer programs. Compare the visual-fit graph in Exhibit 18-13, Panel B, with the least-squares graph in Exhibit 18-13, Panel C. While the graphs look similar, the least-squares method results in a more sophisticated and accurate analysis. In simple terms, the least-squares method minimizes the vertical distance between the equation line and the data points, resulting in a better "fit" of the line to the data.

OBJECTIVE 7 - EVALUATE A MIXED-COST FUNCTION.

Cost functions must be evaluated to determine that they do provide a good explanation for the cost. Two important criteria for evaluating cost functions are economic plausibility and goodness of fit.

Economic plausibility means that a credible cause-and-effect relationship exists between the cost driver and the cost. For example, if the number of work repair orders for an airline increases, total repair costs should also increase.

Goodness of fit means that the relationship between the cost driver and the cost must explain past costs well. In other words, fluctuation in the volume of cost driver activity should be associated with fluctuation in the total cost. Regression analysis provides a goodness of fit statistic called the coefficient of determination. It is represented as r-squared (r^2). An r^2 level of .90 would indicate that 90 percent of the fluctuation in costs is explained by fluctuation in cost driver volume, while a level of .10 would mean that only 10 percent of cost fluctuation is explained by the cost driver.

TEST YOURSELF

All the self-testing materials in this chapter focus on information and procedures that your instructor is likely to test in quizzes and examinations.

I. MATCHING - MATCH EACH NUMBERED TERM WITH ITS LETTERED DEFINITION.

____ 1. committed fixed costs

____ 2. cost function

____ 3. discretionary fixed costs

____ 4. discretionary variable costs

____ 5. engineered variable costs

____ 6. step function variable cost

____ 7. mixed cost

____ 8. work measurement

____ 9. variance

A. capacity costs that managers cannot change in the short run

B. a cost that is a combination of both fixed and variable elements

C. capacity costs that arise from periodic budget decisions and that have no clear relationship between inputs and outputs

D. cost for an input which must be purchased in whole quantities but may be used in fractional quantities

E. costs that result from measurable cause-and-effect relationships between inputs and outputs

F. costs that change with sales or production because of a management decision

G. the careful analysis of a task: its size, the methods used, and its efficiency

H. the mathematical relationship between a cost and its cost driver

I. the difference between an actual amount and the corresponding budgeted amount

II. MULTIPLE CHOICE - CIRCLE THE CORRECT ANSWER.

1. Costs that arise from periodic budget decisions and do not have a clear relationship between inputs and outputs are:

   A. committed fixed costs
   B. discretionary fixed costs
   C. mixed costs
   D. step-function variable costs

2. Belk Co. pays one salesperson a salary of $40,000 and another salesperson a salary of $15,000 plus a commission of $40 per unit sold. At what level of sales will the two salespersons' earnings be equal?

A. 1,000 units
B. 375 units
C. 625 units
D. cannot be determined

3. Which of the following statements about a linear cost function is false?

A. It can be graphed as a straight line.
B. It is either fixed, variable, or mixed.
C. It should not have a negative slope.
D. If the volume of the cost driver doubles, the total amount of cost always doubles.

4. Which method of cost function estimation minimizes the vertical distance between the data points on a graph and the line representing the cost function?

A. high-low
B. visual-fit
C. mixed-cost-formula
D. least-squares regression

Use the following information for questions 5 through 7:

Burgess Taxi Corp. wants to predict the cost of its taxi service. The company has collected the following data:

Month	Miles	Total Cost
January	1,875	$624
February	1,500	461
March	3,800	760
April	2,300	550
May	3,500	624
June	2,700	650

5. Using the high-low method, what is the variable-cost component of the total cost?

A. $0.11
B. $7.69
C. $3.85
D. $0.13

6. Using the high-low method, what is the fixed-cost component of the total cost?

A. $266
B. $299
C. $1,925
D. $375

7. What is the total estimated cost of driving 3,000 miles in a month?

A. $705
B. $23,369
C. $689
D. $656

8. What type of cost is a telephone bill most likely to be?

   A. fixed
   B. variable
   C. step-function
   D. mixed

III. COMPLETION - COMPLETE EACH OF THE FOLLOWING STATEMENTS.

1. Two categories of variable costs are ______________________________

   and ____

2. Fixed costs are ordinarily categorized as either ____________________

   or ____

3. What are the two major assumptions that are the basis of cost functions?

   A. ____

   B. ____

4. Three methods used to estimate mixed-cost functions are:

   A. ____

   B. ____

   C. ____

5. Two important criteria for evaluating cost functions are

   A. ____

   B. ____

IV. EXERCISES

1. Homer Hancock is considering the following three plans for paying his salespeople next year:

   Discretionary-fixed-cost plan: a salary of $40,830.
   Discretionary-variable-cost plan: a commission of $100 per item sold
   Mixed-cost plan: a salary of $23,430 plus a commission of $29 per item sold

   Compute the point of indifference, in terms of items sold, between the discretionary-fixed-cost plan and the mixed-cost plan.

   Compute the point of indifference between the discretionary-variable-cost plan and the mixed-cost plan.

2. Amy Craftner rented a store on the town square to sell craft items. Her rent is $32,500 per year. The average selling price for each item sold is $19.50 and the average variable cost per craft item is $6.50. How many items must Amy sell to break even?

Amy believes that she can sell 13,000 craft items each year if she rents a larger store for $58,500. However, expected demand with a smaller store is now 10,400 items. The smaller store rents for $26,000 annually. Which store should Amy rent?

3. Samuel Smu needs to estimate the cost behavior of one of his client's utility bills. His only sources of data are two monthly bills for last year and the number of machine hours of operation for each of the two months. This data shows:

Machine Hours for the Month	Monthly Utility Costs Incurred
720	$6,660
1,200	$8,100

Use the high-low method to estimate the monthly variable utility cost and the fixed utility cost per machine hour.

Estimate the total utility expense for next month if the plant is expected to operate for 1100 machine hours.

4. Calhoun Chair Co employs 12 workers for 21 eight-hour days each month to assemble lounge chairs. On the basis of a work measurement study, Calhoun's owner budgeted the efficiency of each worker as the rate of two hours per assembled chair. Last month the workers assembled 980 lounge chairs.

   Prepare a performance report using the engineered-variable-cost approach.

   Prepare a performance report using the discretionary-fixed-cost approach.

SOLUTIONS

I. MATCHING

1. A 2. H 3. C 4. F 5. E 6. D 7. B 8. G 9. I

II. MULTIPLE CHOICE

1. B Of the answers given, only discretionary-fixed costs are determined by management decisions.

2. C $40,000 = $15,000 + $40 X units sold

$25,000 = $40 X units sold

625 = units sold

3. D Cost functions are straight lines. Answer D is not correct because the slope will always be zero (all fixed costs) or upwardly sloping (variable or mixed). Costs do not decrease as the activity level increases!

4. D Of answers A, B, and D, only D uses all points in a consistent measurable manner. Answer C is nonsense.

5. D Variable cost per mile = $\frac{\$760 - \$461}{3,800 - 1,500} = \frac{\$299}{2,300} = \$0.13$

6. A Fixed cost = $760 - $0.13 X 3,800 = $266

7. C Total cost = Fixed cost + Variable cost per mile X miles driven

= $266 + $0.13 X 3000 miles

= $656

8. D A telephone bill is comprised of a fixed cost to provide the telephone line and a variable charge for the number of minutes that the phone is used. Alternatively, local service may be a fixed cost while long distance service is a variable cost based on the number and length of calls

III. COMPLETION

1. engineered variable costs and discretionary variable costs
2. committed fixed costs or discretionary fixed costs
3. Cost behavior can be explained by one cost driver.
   The cost function is linear over the relevant range.
4. high-low, visual-fit, and least-squares regression
5. economic plausibility and goodness of fit

IV. EXERCISES

1. Fixed-plan total cost = Mixed-plan total cost

$40,830 = $23,430 + $29 X items sold

600 = Items sold

Variable-plan total cost = Mixed-plan total cost

$100 X items sold = $23,430 + $29 X items sold

330 = Items sold

2.

$$\frac{\text{Fixed Expenses}}{\text{Contribution Margin Per Unit}} = \text{Break-Even in Units}$$

$$\frac{\$32,500}{\$19.50 - \$6.50} = 2500 \text{ units}$$

	Larger Store	Smaller Store
Sales Revenue [1]	$253,500	$202,800
Variable Expenses [2]	84,500	67,600
Contribution margin	$169,000	$135,200
Fixed Expenses [3]	58,500	26,000
Income from operations	$110,000	$109,200

[1] Larger store $19.50 X 13,000 items = $253,500
Smaller store $19.50 X 10,400 items = $202,800

[2] Larger store $6.50 X 13,000 items = $84,500
Smaller store $6.50 X 10,400 items = $67,600

[3] Larger store rent $58,500
Smaller store rent $26,000

Amy should rent the larger store.

3. Variable expenses (as a proportion of sales) = Change in utility costs / Change in machine hours

$$VC = \frac{\$8{,}100 - \$6{,}660}{1200\text{ MH} - 720\text{ MH}} = \frac{\$1{,}440}{480\text{ MH}} = \$3 / \text{MH}$$

Fixed expenses = Total expenses - Variable expenses

= $8,100 - 1200 MH X $3

= $4,500

OR

= $6,660 - 720 MH X $3

= $4,500

Total costs = Fixed costs + Variable costs

= $4,500 + 1,100 MH X $3

= $7,800

4.

$$\text{Unit cost} = \frac{\text{Monthly salary}}{\text{Chairs assembled per month}} = \frac{\$1{,}200}{(8\text{ hr X }21\text{ day}) / 2\text{ hr per chair}}$$

= $15 per chair

	Budget as an Engineered Variable Cost	Actual Cost	Variance: Amount	Variance: Equivalent Persons
Salaries	$18,300 [1]	$18,000 [2]	$300 [f]	.25 [3]

[1] 1220 chairs X $15
[2] 15 workers X $1,200
[f] Favorable (actual costs are less than budget)
[3] $300 / $1,200 = .25 salaries

	Budget as a Discretionary Fixed Cost	Actual Cost	Variance
Salaries	$18,000	$18,000	$ -0-

DEMONSTRATION PROBLEM 1

Part A

Cohoma Chemical makes and sells agricultural chemicals in Clarksdale, Mississippi. Ross Smith, the owner, is considering two alternatives for paying his two salespersons next year (19X8). Plan A is a straight commission of $0.888 per gallon sold. Plan B is a salary of $44,400 each plus a commission of $0.444 per gallon.

REQUIRED:

1. Graph the cost behavior of both plans.

2. Determine both graphically and with equations the number of gallons the sales force would have to sell for Ross to pay the same total compensation under both plans.

Part B

During 19X7, Ross operated at full capacity of 888,000 gallons. Each salesperson was paid according to Plan A above. The average sales price was $22.20 per gallon, and the average variable cost (excluding commissions) was $13.32 per gallon. Fixed expenses totaled $2,220,000.

Ross believes that his salespersons can sell 1,110,000 gallons in 19X8 and every year thereafter if his company can produce them. He estimates an additional committed fixed cost of $444,000 would be required to provide the additional capacity.

REQUIRED:

1. Compute 19X8 operating income on a contribution-margin income statement if Ross acquires the additional capacity and produces and sells 1,110,000 gallons. Assume ross Switches to Plan B (a salary of $44,400 each and commission of $0.444 per gallon) to pay salespersons.

2. Repeat Requirement 1 assuming Ross continues to pay compensation according to Plan A (a straight commission of $0.888 per gallon).

DEMONSTRATION PROBLEM 2

John Owens, the delivery manager of Delicious Delights, needs a cost function to predict delivery department costs. He believes the primary cost driver is the number of deliveries made. John collected the following observations for the most recent six months of activity:

Month	Number of Deliveries	Total Cost
1	3,500	$6,500
2	3,400	6,410
3	3,700	7,000
4	2,500	5,780
5	2,000	5,420
6	4,500	7,200

REQUIRED:

1. Plot the data observations, with total delivery department cost as the dependent variable (y) and the number of deliveries as the independent variable (x).

2. Regression analysis reveals that the equation of the best-fitting straight line through the sample points is:

   Total cost = $3930 + $0.752 per delivery

   Draw the regression analysis line on the graph.

3. Use the high-low method to estimate the cost function. Draw the high-low line on the graph, and compare the high-low equation with the regression equation.

4. Use both the high-low and regression analysis cost functions to predict delivery department cost for a month in which John makes 4,100 deliveries to customers.

19

Manufacturing Accounting And Job Order Costing

CHAPTER REVIEW

Identify the dual objectives of a cost accounting system.

A business must aim to control the total costs of the company -- the cost of all functions in the value chain as a whole. The value chain includes research, product development, manufacturing, marketing, distribution, and customer service costs.

The primary objectives of a cost accounting system are cost control and product costing. The objective of cost control is to produce the maximum amount of output (finished product) at a minimum cost. The objective of product costing is to measure the value of inventory, cost of goods sold, and profitability. Product costing is important because in the long term a business must be able to earn a profit in order to continue operating.

OBJECTIVE 1 - PREPARE THE FINANCIAL STATEMENTS OF A MANUFACTURING COMPANY.

Merchandisers have one inventory--the products they sell. Manufacturers have three inventories--raw materials, work in process, and finished goods.

Raw materials inventory is the material used to manufacture the finished goods. Work in process inventory tracks the cost of goods which have been put into the manufacturing process but have not yet been completed. Finished goods inventory is the final products which are ready to be sold.

Inventory accounts are the only difference between the balance sheet of a merchandiser and that of a manufacturer. Study Exhibit 19-2 in your text to be sure you understand the difference.

Cost of goods manufactured is the manufacturer's counterpart to the merchandiser's Purchases account. This is the only difference between a manufacturer's income statement and a merchandiser's income statement. Study Exhibit 19-3 in your text to be sure you understand the difference.

OBJECTIVE 2 - COMPUTE COST OF GOODS MANUFACTURED.

Manufacturing terms:

Direct materials (1) become a physical part of the finished product and (2) are separately and conveniently traceable to finished goods.

Direct labor is the cost of salaries and wages of the employees who physically convert materials into finished goods.

Factory overhead includes all manufacturing costs except direct materials and direct labor.

Indirect materials are materials used to manufacture a product that are not conveniently traceable to specific finished products. The cost of indirect materials is accounted for as part of factory overhead.

Indirect labor consists of the wages and salaries of all factory workers who are not directly involved in converting material into finished goods. The cost of indirect labor is accounted for as part of factory overhead.

Prime costs are the sum of direct materials plus direct labor.

Conversion costs are the sum of direct labor plus factory overhead.

Computing cost of goods manufactured:

(1) Direct materials used = beginning raw materials + purchases - ending raw materials

(2) Total manufacturing costs = direct materials used + direct labor + factory overhead

(3) Cost of goods manufactured = beginning work in process + total manufacturing costs - ending work in process

Familiarize yourself with Exhibit 19-4 to be sure you understand how to compute cost of goods manufactured.

Study the diagram below. It will help you to understand the flow of inventory costs through a manufacturing company.

DIRECT MATERIALS	**WORK IN PROCESS**	**FINISHED GOODS**
Beginning inventory	Beginning inventory	Beginning inventory
+ Purchases	+ Direct materials used	+ Cost of goods manufactured
	+ Direct labor	
	+ Factory overhead	
Direct materials available for use	Subtotal	Goods available for sale
- Ending inventory	- Ending inventory	- Ending inventory
Direct materials used	Cost of goods manufactured	Cost of goods sold

Note that all of the costs which flow through manufacturing inventories are called product costs. If a cost is associated with the manufacturing process, it is a product cost.

Period costs are not traced through the inventory accounts. They are accounted for as operating expenses and include selling expenses and general and administrative expenses.

OBJECTIVE 3 - USE JOB ORDER COSTING INFORMATION.

Job order costing accounts for products produced as (1) individual units or (2) distinct batches of products. A job can be a single unit of a product (one airplane) or a distinct batch of similar units of a product (10 sofas).

Costs are recorded and summarized on a job cost record (Exhibit 19-7).

OBJECTIVE 4 - ACCOUNT FOR MATERIALS IN A JOB ORDER COSTING SYSTEM.

A manufacturer acquires materials by sending a purchase order to a supplier. When the materials are received, a receiving report is prepared and a journal entry is recorded:

Materials Inventory	XX	
Accounts Payable		XX

A subsidiary materials ledger is maintained which tracks the receipt, usage, and balance of each materials inventory item.

When a job is entered into production, a materials requisition is prepared to have materials transferred from inventory storage to the factory floor.

The cost of direct materials is debited to Work in Process Inventory, while the cost of any indirect materials is debited to Factory Overhead:

Work in Process	XX	
Factory Overhead	XX	
Materials Inventory		XX

This entry records the transfer of materials from inventory to the manufacturing process. At the same time, the cost of the **direct** materials is entered on the job cost record.

OBJECTIVE 5 - ACCOUNT FOR LABOR IN A JOB ORDER COSTING SYSTEM.

A labor time ticket (Exhibit 19-11 in your text) is used to accumulate the time spent on a job and the labor cost associated with the job.

Factory wages are recorded with this entry:

Factory Wages	XX	
Wages Payable		XX

Based on the information from the labor time tickets, the balance in the Factory Wages account is allocated to direct labor and indirect labor, and recorded with this entry:

Work in Process Inventory	XX	
Factory Overhead	XX	
Factory Wages		XX

The direct labor costs associated with each job are posted to the appropriate job cost records.

OBJECTIVE 6 - ACCOUNT FOR OVERHEAD IN A JOB ORDER COSTING SYSTEM.

During the year, overhead costs are debited to Factory Overhead as they are incurred:

Factory Overhead	XX
Various Accounts	XX

At year end, the Factory Overhead contains all the actual overhead costs of the period. Our task now is to determine how to apply these overhead costs to the products that were produced. However, applying overhead costs to production cannot wait until the end of each year. Accountants usually compute a budgeted factory overhead rate so that overhead can be applied during the year:

$$\text{BUDGETED FACTORY OVERHEAD RATE} = \frac{\text{BUDGETED TOTAL OVERHEAD}}{\text{TOTAL BUDGETED COST APPLICATION BASE}}$$

The cost application base is likely to be (1) budgeted direct labor dollars, (2) budgeted direct labor hours, or (3) budgeted machine hours.

Overhead is applied using the budgeted overhead rate on a uniform basis throughout the year. For example, if overhead is applied at the rate of 80% of direct labor dollars, and direct labor dollars are $500, then applied overhead is $500 X 80% or $400.

The entry to record application of overhead is:

Work in Process Inventory	XX
Factory Overhead	XX

Once overhead is applied to a job, we can compute unit cost:

$$\text{UNIT COST} = \frac{\text{DIRECT MATERIALS + DIRECT LABOR + OVERHEAD APPLIED}}{\text{NUMBER OF UNITS PRODUCED}}$$

As jobs are completed, they are transferred to finished goods:

Finished Goods Inventory	XX
Work in Process Inventory	XX

When goods are sold, these entries are recorded:

Accounts Receivable	XX
Sales Revenue	XX
Cost of Goods Sold	XX
Finished Goods Inventory	XX

Note: The difference in these 2 entries represents gross profit.

Consider this T-account:

Factory Overhead	
Actual	Applied

If applied overhead is less than actual overhead (a debit balance remains), then overhead is <u>underapplied</u>. If applied overhead is greater than actual overhead (a credit balance remains), then overhead is <u>overapplied</u>.

Insignificant amounts of over- or underapplied overhead are closed to Cost of Goods Sold at year end. Significant amounts of over- or underapplied overhead are allocated to Work in Process, Finished Goods, and Cost of Goods Sold.

TEST YOURSELF

All the self-testing materials in this chapter focus on information and procedures that your instructor is likely to test in quizzes and examinations.

I. MATCHING - MATCH EACH NUMBERED TERM WITH ITS LETTERED DEFINITION.

____ 1. budgeted factory overhead rate

____ 2. direct labor

____ 3. direct materials

____ 4. factory overhead

____ 5. indirect materials

____ 6. indirect labor

____ 7. job order cost

____ 8. job cost record

____ 9. period costs

____10. product cost

____11. labor time ticket

____12. materials inventory

____13. materials requisition

____14. overapplied overhead

____15. total manufacturing cost

____16. underapplied overhead

____17. work in process inventory

____18. finished goods inventory

A. A document that identifies the amount of time the employee spent on a particular job

B. A debit balance remaining in the Factory Overhead account after overhead is applied

C. A document prepared by manufacturing personnel requesting materials to be used in production

D. A document used to accumulate and control cost in a job order system

E. All manufacturing costs other than direct materials and direct labor

F. An accounting system used by companies that manufacture products as individual units or in batches

G. Any cost identified with goods manufactured for sale

H. Budgeted total overhead divided by the budgeted rate base

I. Completed goods that have not yet been sold

J. Cost of salaries and wages for the employees who physically convert materials into the company's products

K. Costs which are never traced through the inventory accounts

L. Factory labor costs which are difficult to trace to specific products

M. Goods that are in production but not complete at the end of the period

N. Manufacturing materials with costs that cannot easily be traced to a particular finished product

O. Material that becomes a physical part of a finished product and whose cost is separately and conveniently traceable through the manufacturing process to finished goods

P. Materials on hand to be used in the manufacturing process

Q. Results when applied overhead exceeds the actual overhead cost

R. Sum of direct materials used, direct labor, and factory overhead

II. MULTIPLE CHOICE - CIRCLE THE CORRECT ANSWER.

1. If cost of goods manufactured exceeds total manufacturing costs, which of the following is always true?

   A. finished goods inventory has increased
   B. finished goods inventory has decreased
   C. work in process inventory has decreased
   D. work in process inventory has increased

2. If finished goods inventory has increased, which of the following is always true?

   A. total manufacturing costs are more than cost of goods manufactured
   B. total manufacturing costs are less than cost of goods manufactured
   C. cost of goods sold is less than cost of goods manufactured
   D. cost of goods sold is more than cost of goods manufactured

3. Which of the following manufacturers would be least likely to use process costing?

   A. oil refinery
   B. contractors
   C. aircraft
   D. furniture

4. When indirect materials are used in production:

   A. Work in Process is debited
   B. Factory Overhead is credited
   C. Factory Overhead is debited
   D. Materials is debited

5. When direct materials are used in production:

   A. Work is Process is credited
   B. Factory Overhead is debited
   C. Materials is debited
   D. Work in Process is debited

6. When factory wages are allocated, indirect labor is:

   A. debited to Work in Process
   B. debited to Factory Overhead
   C. credited to Factory Overhead
   D. credited to Work in Process

7. The entry to debit Cost of Goods Sold and credit Finished Goods as sales are made is recorded in:

   A. a periodic inventory system
   B. a perpetual inventory system
   C. both a periodic inventory system and a perpetual inventory system
   D. neither a periodic inventory system nor a perpetual inventory system

8. Underapplied overhead implies:

   A. a credit balance in the Factory Overhead account
   B. a debit balance in the Factory Overhead account
   C. too much overhead was applied
   D. Cost of Goods sold is overstated

III. COMPLETION - COMPLETE EACH OF THE FOLLOWING STATEMENTS.

1. The dual objectives of a cost accounting system are:

   ______________________________ and ______________________________.

2. The inventory accounts of a manufacturing firm will include:

   ______________________________, ______________________________, and

   ______________________________.

3. ______________________________ are a physical part of the finished product and their cost is separately and conveniently traceable through the manufacturing process.

4. Indirect materials and indirect labor are part of ______________________________

   ______________________________.

5. ______________________________ are also called inventoriable costs.

6. ______________________________ are never traced through the inventory accounts.

7. There are two main types of accounting systems for product costing:

   ______________________________ and ______________________________.

IV. EXERCISES

1. If Cost of Goods Manufactured was $160,000, and beginning and ending work in process inventories were $10,000 and $12,000 respectively, what were Total Manufacturing Costs?

2. Work In Process inventory increased $600 during the year for a manufacturing company. Total manufacturing costs were $32,000. What was Cost of Goods Manufactured?

3. The following depreciation schedule is given:

Factory Building	$40,000
Sales Office	30,000
Factory Equipment	16,000
Salesmen's Automobiles	8,000

How much depreciation should be included in Factory Overhead?

4. The following information pertains to Wooden Toys, Inc. for 19X9:

Cost of Goods Sold	$280,000
Direct Materials Purchased	125,000
Direct Materials Used	126,250
Ending Work in Process	
Less Beginning Work in Process	11,250

Finished Goods Inventory did not change.
Factory Overhead is twice direct labor cost.
Beginning Work in Process is 40% of Ending Work in Process.

A. Compute Beginning and Ending Work in Process.

B. Compute Cost of Goods Manufactured.

C. Compute Total Manufacturing Costs.

D. Compute Direct Labor and Factory Overhead.

5. The following information pertains to Penny's Peanut Brittle Co. for 19X0:

Actual Factory Overhead	$41,000
Actual direct labor cost	21,000
Budgeted direct labor cost for the year	20,000
Overapplied overhead	5,000

A. How much overhead was applied in 19X0?

B. What was the budgeted overhead application rate?

SOLUTIONS

I. MATCHING

1. H	2. J	3. O	4. E	5. N	6. L	7. F	8. D	9. K	10. G
11. A	12. P	13. C	14. Q	15. R	16. B	17. M	18. I		

II. MULTIPLE CHOICE

1. C Recall:

    Beginning Work In Process
    + Total Manufacturing Costs
    - Ending Work In Process
    = Cost of Goods Manufactured

    If the cost of goods manufactured exceeds total manufacturing costs, then the effect on WIP inventory must be positive. Accordingly, beginning WIP must be greater than ending WIP inventory. If the ending balance is smaller that the beginning balance, the inventory has decreased.

2. C Recall:

    Beginning Finished Goods Inventory
    + Cost of Goods Manufactured
    = Goods Available for Sale
    - Ending Finished Goods Iventory
    = Cost of Goods Sold

    If finished goods inventory has increased, the net effect of finished goods on the above formula is negative. Accordingly, Cost of Goods Sold would be less that Cost of Goods Manufactured. Answers A and B are incorrect because they do not relate to the finished goods account.

3. A Process costing is used by manufacturers producing a continuous flow of the same product. Of the manufacturers listed, the oil refinery is least likely to produce the same product in a continuous flow.

4. C The use of indirect materials requires Materials Inventory to be reduced and Factory Overhead to be increased. The journal entry is:

Factory Overhead	XX	
Materials Inventory		XX

5. D The journal entry for the use of Direct Materials is:

Work in Process Inventory	XX	
Materials Inventory		XX

6. B Recall that factory wages are cleared through a clearing account so that direct and indirect labor can be allocated properly. In recording the payroll allocation, Work in Process Inventory is debited for direct labor and Factory Overhead is debited for indirect labor.

7. B Only a perpetual inventory system has a Cost of Goods Sold account.

III. COMPLETION

1. cost control, product costing
2. materials, work in process, finished goods
3. direct materials
4. factory overhead
5. product costs
6. period costs
7. job order costing, process costing

IV. EXERCISES

1.

Beginning Work In Process	$ 10,000
+ Total Manufacturing Costs	?
- Ending Work In Process	12,000
= Cost of Goods Manufactured	$160,000

Total Manufacturing Costs = $158,000

2.

Beginning Work In Process	$ X
+ Total Manufacturing Costs	32,000
- Ending Work In Process	X + 600
= Cost of Goods Manufactured	$?

X + $32,000 - (X + $600) = $31,400

3.

Factory Building	$40,000
Factory Equipment	16,000
	$56,000

4. A. End. WIP - Beg. WIP = $11,250
Beg. WIP = .4 X End. WIP

End. WIP - .4 X End. WIP = $11,250
End. WIP = $18,750

Beg. WIP = .4 X $18,750 = $7,500

B. Beg. FG + Cost of Goods Manu. - End. FG = COGS
Beg. FG = End. FG
Cost of Goods Manufactured = COGS = $280,000

C.

Beginning Work in Process	$ 7,500
+ Total Manufacturing Costs	X
- Ending Work in Process	18,750
= Cost of Goods Manufactured	$280,000

Total Manufacturing Costs = $291,250

D.

Direct Materials Used	$126,250
+ Direct Labor	X
+ Overhead	2X
= Total Manufacturing Costs	$291,250

5. A. Applied Overhead - Actual Overhead = Overapplied overhead

X - $41,000 = $ 5,200

X = $46,200

B. Overhead rate X Actual Direct Labor cost = Overhead applied

OH rate X $21,000 = $46,200

OH rate = 220% Direct Labor cost

DEMONSTRATION PROBLEM

Billie Goat had the following inventory balances on January 1, 19X0:

Materials	$60,000
Work in Process	26,015
Finished Goods	37,650

During the month of January 19X0, he completed the following transactions:

A. Billie purchased 1,500 tons of used newspapers (materials) for $25 per ton.

B. His workers requisitioned $50,000 of direct materials.

C. $2,760 of indirect materials were used.

D. He incurred $16,000 in factory wages (75% was direct labor).

E. He incurred the following additional overhead costs:
   1. $700 in depreciation on factory equipment
   2. $5,315 in miscellaneous other costs (credit Accounts Payable)

F. Overhead is applied to production at the rate of 25% of direct materials cost.

G. Three orders were completed. The total cost of these orders was $87,725.

H. Billie sold four orders on account. The total cost of these orders was $109,290. The total sales price for the orders was $153,060.

I. Factory Overhead was closed to Cost of Goods Sold.

REQUIRED:

1. Record the transactions in the general journal.

2. What were the ending balances in the inventory accounts?

3. Was Factory Overhead overapplied or underapplied?

4. What will be the amount of Cost of Goods Sold on the January income statement?

Requirement 1 (record transactions)

GENERAL JOURNAL

Account	PR	Debit	Credit

Factory Overhead account:

Factory Overhead	

Requirement 2 (inventory balances)

Materials	

Work in Process	

Finished Goods	

Requirement 3 (overhead)

Factory overhead is ______________________________.

Requirement 4 (cost of goods sold)

Cost of Goods Sold	

20

Process Costing

CHAPTER REVIEW

OBJECTIVE 1 - DISTINGUISH PROCESS COSTING FROM JOB ORDER COSTING.

<u>Process costing</u> assigns costs to goods produced in a continuous sequence of steps called processes. With process costing, costs are accumulated for a period of time, such as a week or a month. This contrasts with a job order cost system, which accounts for costs of specific batches of product.

With process costing, a product typically passes through several departments. For each department, there is a separate Work in Process Inventory account. (In a job order costing system, there is one Work in Process Inventory account supported by job cost records for the various jobs.) Process costing typically accounts for <u>direct materials</u> and <u>conversion costs</u>. Recall that conversion costs represent the sum of direct labor plus factory overhead.

The journal entries used for process costing are very similar to those used for job order costing. One major difference is that when goods are transferred from one department to the next, the costs are also transferred from one Work in Process Inventory account to another:

Work in Process Inventory - Dept. 2	XX	
Work in Process Inventory - Dept. 1		XX

Additional materials and conversion costs may be added in subsequent departments.

OBJECTIVE 2 - COMPUTE EQUIVALENT UNITS OF PRODUCTION.

and

OBJECTIVE 3 - APPLY TOTAL COST TO UNITS COMPLETED AND UNITS IN ENDING WORK IN PROCESS INVENTORY.

The task in process costing is to account for both the cost of goods that have been completed as well as the cost of incomplete units.

<u>Equivalent units of production</u> are the number of complete units that <u>could</u> have been manufactured from start to finish using the costs incurred during the period.

$$\text{EQUIVALENT UNITS OF PRODUCTION} = \text{UNITS COMPLETED DURING THE PERIOD} + \left[\text{PARTIALLY COMPLETE UNITS} \times \text{PERCENTAGE OF COMPLETION}\right]$$

If there is no beginning Work in Process inventory, use the following steps to apply process costing:

Step 1 Total physical units <u>to account for</u> = beginning work in process + production started during the period.

Total physical units accounted for = units completed and transferred out during the period + ending Work in Process.

Units to account for should always equal units accounted for.

Step 2 Compute equivalent units of production separately for direct materials and conversion costs. Remember that this is necessary because the percentage of completion may be different for materials and conversion costs. Turn to Exhibit 20-3 in your text to review Steps 1 and 2.

Step 3 Summarize total cost to account for. Total costs to account for = cost of beginning work in process + direct materials + direct labor + factory overhead. This is equal to the balance in the Work in Process account for the department. Review Exhibit 20-4.

Step 4 Compute separate unit costs for direct materials and conversion costs:

$$\text{UNIT COSTS} = \frac{\text{COSTS ADDED DURING THE PERIOD}}{\text{EQUIVALENT UNITS}}$$

TOTAL COST PER UNIT	=	UNIT COST FOR DIRECT MATERIALS	+	UNIT COST FOR CONVERSION

Step 5 The unit costs from Step 4 are applied to units completed and to units in ending Work in Process.

Cost of units completed and transferred out = units completed and transferred out X total unit costs.

Cost of ending work in process = (equivalent units of ending work in process for direct materials X unit cost for direct materials) + (equivalent units of ending work in process for conversion X unit cost for conversion).

Review Exhibit 20-6. Note that the total costs accounted for in Step 5 must agree with the total cost from Step 3.

OBJECTIVE 4 - RECORD PROCESS COSTING TRANSACTIONS.

To record current period costs:

Work in Process Inventory - Dept. 1	XX	
Materials Inventory		XX
Work in Process Inventory - Dept. 1	XX	
Factory Wages		XX
Work in Process Inventory - Dept. 1	XX	
Factory Overhead		XX

To record the transfer to the next department:

Work in Process Inventory - Dept. 2	XX	
Work in Process Inventory - Dept. 1		XX

OBJECTIVE 5 - ACCOUNT FOR PROCESS COSTING IN A SECOND DEPARTMENT USING THE FIFO METHOD.

When working with multiple departments, it is important to distinguish between costs from the prior department and costs in the current department. Remember that the costs follow the units from department to department.

All costs in a department which were incurred in prior departments are called <u>transferred-in costs</u>. Only costs in the current department are accounted for as material or conversion costs in that department.

When beginning Work in Process Inventory exists and the FIFO (first-in, first-out) method is used, certain changes occur in the five steps used in the application of process costing:

Step 1 With a second department, units started are replaced by units transferred in. This follows the flow of production in physical units.

Total units to account for = beginning work in process + units transferred in.

Total units accounted for = units from beginning work in process completed and transferred out + units transferred in, completed, and transferred out during the current period + ending work in process.

Note that total units to account for should be equal to total units accounted for. Note also that the FIFO method requires the separation of completed units into units from beginning inventory and units started and completed during the period.

Step 2 When computing equivalent units, there are three categories: transferred-in equivalent units, direct materials equivalent units, and conversion equivalent units. For each category, equivalent units are computed for (1) units from beginning inventory that were completed and transferred out, (2) units started (transferred in) and completed during the period, and (3) units in ending inventory.

Note that equivalent units for units completed from beginning inventory is equal to the percentage of work done during the current month (subtract the percentage completed during the prior month from 100%).

Study Exhibit 20-8 in your text to be sure you understand equivalent unit computations in a multiple department FIFO process cost system.

Steps 3, 4, and 5 are similar to what is done for a single department with no beginning inventory. When performing Step 4, remember that costs associated with beginning Work in Process are **NOT** included in the unit cost calculation.

The journal entries to record costs in a second department are:

Work in Process Inventory - Dept. 2	XX	
Materials Inventory		XX
Work in Process Inventory - Dept. 2	XX	
Factory Wages		XX
Work in Process Inventory - Dept. 2	XX	
Factory Overhead		XX

The journal entry to record the transfer of completed units to Finished Goods Inventory is:

Finished Goods Inventory	XX	
Work in Process Inventory - Dept. 2		XX

OBJECTIVE 6 - ACCOUNT FOR PROCESS COSTING IN A SECOND DEPARTMENT USING THE WEIGHTED AVERAGE METHOD.

When beginning Work in Process Inventory exists, certain differences exist between the weighted average method and the FIFO method of process costing. These differences (**highlighted**) occur because costs from the current period are averaged in with costs from the prior period:

Step 1 With a second department, units started are replaced by units transferred in. This follows the flow of production in physical units.

Total units to account for = beginning work in process + units transferred in.

Total units accounted for = units transferred out during the current period + ending work in process.

The total units to account for should still be equal to total units accounted for. **Note also that the weighted-average method does not require the separation of completed units into units from beginning inventory and units started and completed during the period.**

Step 2 When computing equivalent units, there are three categories: transferred-in equivalent units, direct materials equivalent units, and conversion equivalent units. For each category, equivalent units are computed for **(1) units transferred out, and (2) units in ending inventory.**

Study Exhibit 20-13 in your text to be sure you understand equivalent unit computations in a multiple department weighted-average process cost system.

Steps 3, 4, and 5 are similar to what is done for a single department with no beginning inventory. When performing Step 4, remember that costs associated with beginning Work in Process **are** included in the unit cost calculation.

The journal entries to record costs in a second department are the same for both FIFO and weighted-average (only the dollar amounts will differ).

TEST YOURSELF

All the self-testing materials in this chapter focus on information and procedures that your instructor is likely to test in quizzes and examinations.

I. MATCHING - MATCH EACH NUMBERED TERM WITH ITS LETTERED DEFINITION.

____ 1. transferred-in costs

____ 2. equivalent units

____ 3. FIFO method

____ 4. weighted average method

____ 5. conversion cost

____ 6. unit costs

____ 7. production cost report

A. Method with only two categories of physical units

B. Measure of the number of complete units that could have been manufactured from start to finish using the costs incurred during the period

C. Costs incurred in all previous departments

D. Costs for a category divided by the equivalent units for the same category

E. Summary of the activity in a processing department for a period

F. The sum of direct labor and overhead

G. Method that focuses on the current period

II. MULTIPLE CHOICE - CIRCLE THE CORRECT ANSWER.

1. When using FIFO for unit cost calculations in process costing, the numerator (costs) and the denominator (equivalent units) include:

   A. Current amounts only for both
   B. Current amounts only for the numerator and current and beginning amounts for the denominator
   C. Current and beginning amounts for the numerator and current amounts only for the denominator
   D. Current and beginning amounts for both the numerator and denominator

2. All of the following businesses are likely to use a process costing system except:

   A. industrial chemicals
   B. paint
   C. residential construction
   D. soft drinks

3. The journal entry to assign labor costs in a process costing system would:

   A. credit Factory Wages
   B. credit Work in Process Inventory
   C. credit Finished Goods
   D. debit Factory Wages

4. The journal entry transferring costs from Department A to Department B in a process costing system would:

   A. debit Work in Process - Department A
   B. credit Work in Process - Department B
   C. debit Work in Process - Department B and credit Work in Process - Department A
   D. debit Work in Process Department A and credit Work in Process - Department B

5. Which of the following systems will have more than one Work in Process account?

   A. job order costing
   B. process costing
   C. both job order costing and process costing
   D. job order costing and process costing both have only one Work in Process account

6. Direct materials in the second department refer to:

   A. materials added in the first department
   B. materials added in the second department
   C. materials added in both departments
   D. materials added in departments other than the first or second

7. When using weighted average for unit cost calculations in process costing, the numerator (costs) and the denominator (equivalent units) include:

   A. Current amounts only for both
   B. Current amounts only for the numerator and current and beginning amounts for the denominator
   C. Current and beginning amounts for the numerator and current amounts only for the denominator
   D. Current and beginning amounts for both the numerator and denominator

III. COMPLETION - COMPLETE EACH OF THE FOLLOWING STATEMENTS.

1. A manufacturer who produces custom goods uses a ______________________ cost system.

2. A manufacturer with a continuous mass production of identical units through a sequence of steps uses a ______________________ cost system.

3. Conversion costs refer to ______________________________________ and ______________________________________.

4. Ending work in process of 5,000 units one-fourth complete would represent ______________________ equivalent units.

5. Ending work in process of 8,000 units with one-fifth of the work left to complete would represent ____________________ equivalent units.

IV. EXERCISES

1. The following information is for Department 1 of Kim's Chemical Co. for the month of June:

Beginning Work in Process Inventory (30% complete as to conversion)	5,000
Units completed and transferred to Dept. 2	40,000
Units in ending Work in Process Inventory (40% complete as to conversion)	10,000

All materials are added at the beginning of Dept. 1.

A. How many physical units were started into production in June?

B. What is the number of equivalent units for materials in June?

C. What is the number of equivalent units for conversion in June?

2. Sansco Industries prepared the following production cost report for Department 1 for February:

	Physical Units	Total Costs
Work in Process February 1 (100% complete as to materials and 40% complete as to conversion)	1,000	$ 6,320
Started into production in February (costs include $95,000 for materials and $68,080 for conversion)	19,000	163,080
Total to account for	20,000	$169,400
Completed and transferred to Department 2 during February	16,000	?
Work in Process, February 28 (100% complete as to materials and 70% complete as to conversion)	4,000	?
Total accounted for	20,000	$169,400

A. What is the cost per equivalent unit for materials?

B. What is the cost per equivalent unit for conversion?

C. What costs are transferred to Department 2 at the end of February?

D. What costs remain in Ending Work in Process Inventory for Department 1?

SOLUTIONS

I. MATCHING

1. C 2. B 3. G 4. A 5. F 6. D 7. E

II. MULTIPLE CHOICE

1. A — When computing unit costs, the costs from the prior period are <u>not included</u> in the computation of unit costs. The unit cost for each cost category is equal to the costs added to that category during the current period divided by the equivalent units for that category.

2. C — Since residential construction tends to be of identifiable units, job order costing would be appropriate for it. Process costing is appropriate for the others listed.

3. A — The entry to assign direct labor costs in a process costing system would be:

Work in Process Inventory - Dept. C	XX	
Factory Wages		XX

4. C — The materials, labor, and overhead costs accumulated as Work in Process Inventory in Dept. A would be transferred to Dept. B with the following journal entry:

Work in Process Inventory - Dept. B	XX	
Work in Process Inventory - Dept. B		XX

5. B — Job order cost systems maintain only one Work in Process Inventory account. The job cost record for each incomplete job in such a system comprises the job cost or work in process subsidiary ledger for the control account. In a process cost system, with more than one department, each department has its own Work in Process Inventory account.

6. B — Materials added in the first department and transferred to the second department are referred to as Transferred-in Costs. Accordingly, only materials added in the current department are called direct materials.

7. D — The weighted average method combines costs associated with beginning inventory and costs incurred during the current period. It also assumes that all work was done in the current period for goods transferred out.

III. COMPLETION

1. job order
2. process
3. direct labor, overhead
4. 1/4 X 5,000 units = 1250
5. (1 - 1/5) X 8,000 units = 6,400

IV. EXERCISES

1. A. Units transferred out + Ending inventory = Units accounted for
   40,000 + 10,000 = 50,000

   Beginning inventory - Units started = Units to account for
   5,000 - X = 50,000
   Units started = 45,000

   B. Equivalent units for materials = units started = 45,000

   C.

Transferred out	40,000
+ Ending inventory (40% X 10,000)	+ 4,000
- Beginning inventory (30% X 5,000)	- 1,500
Equivalent units for conversion	42,500

2. A. Equivalent units for materials = 19,000

   Cost per equivalent unit for materials = $95,000 / 19,000 = $5.00

   B. Equivalent units for conversion = 16,000 + (70% X 4,000) - (40% X 1,000) = 18,400

   Cost per equivalent unit = $68,080 / 18,400 = $3.70

   C.

Cost of beginning Work in Process inventory	$ 6,320
Cost to complete (1,000 X 60% X $3.70)	2,220
Units started and finished [15,000 X ($5.00 + $3.70)]	130,500
Costs transferred out	$139,040

   D.

Materials (4,000 X 100% X $5.00)	$20,000
Conversion (4,000 X 70% X $3.70)	10,360
Cost of Ending Work in Process	$30,360

DEMONSTRATION PROBLEM

Rabbit Egg Works produces decorative eggs. The following is a summary of activity and costs for the coloring department for the month of April:

Coloring Department
For the Month Ended April 30, 19XX

Units:	
Beginning Work in Process Inventory (20% complete as to materials; 40% complete as to conversion)	30,000
Transferred in from the Boiling Department	140,000
Total eggs completed	120,000
Ending Work in Process Inventory (40% complete as to materials; 50% complete as to conversion)	50,000
Costs:	
Beginning Work in Process	
Transferred-In	$ 48,400
Materials	2,240
Conversion	$ 23,270
	$ 73,910
Transferred-in costs from the Boiling Department	210,000
Materials added	18,760
Conversion costs added	273,980

REQUIRED:

1. Show the application of total cost to units completed and units in ending Work in Process Inventory for the Coloring Department for the month of April using the FIFO method.

2. Show the application of total cost to units completed and units in ending Work in Process Inventory for the Coloring Department for the month of April using the weighted-average method.

21

Flexible Budgets And Standard Costs

CHAPTER REVIEW

OBJECTIVE 1 - PREPARE A FLEXIBLE BUDGET FOR THE INCOME STATEMENT.

Cost behavior may be fixed or variable. Mixed costs have both variable and fixed components. Cost behaviors are valid only for a relevant range of activity.

A static budget is prepared for only one level of activity. The static budget is used to budget unit costs and overhead rates. A performance report compares actual with budgeted results to show the variance (difference) and whether the variance is favorable or unfavorable.

A flexible (or variable) budget is a set of budgets covering a range of different sales volumes. Generally, the flexible budget is prepared for actual volume achieved (that is, when actual volume is known).

To prepare a flexible budget, we use the budget formula to compute the budget amounts:

REVENUES - VARIABLE EXPENSES - FIXED EXPENSES = OPERATING INCOME (or LOSS)

[UNITS SOLD X UNIT SALE PRICE] - [UNITS SOLD X VARIABLE COST PER UNIT] - FIXED EXPENSES = OPERATING INCOME (or LOSS)

Note that fixed expenses remain constant. They do not change while the firm operates within the relevant range.

Study Exhibit 21-1 in your text to understand the preparation of a flexible budget income statement.

Graphing the expense formula provides a budget for any level of volume. The vertical axis of the budget expense graph shows total expenses, and the horizontal axis shows the level of volume. Both budgeted and actual results can be graphed. Remember that the only valid portion of the graph is the area within the relevant range. Refer to Exhibits 21-2 and 21-3 in your text for a graph of a flexible expense budget and a graph of actual and budgeted total expenses.

OBJECTIVE 2 - PREPARE AN INCOME STATEMENT PERFORMANCE REPORT.

An income statement performance report is a five-column report:

Column 1 contains actual results at actual prices.

Column 3 contains the flexible budget for actual volume achieved (prepared using the budget formula).

Column 5 contains the static (master) budget.

Column 2 contains flexible budget variances. Flexible budget variances are differences between actual results (Column 1) and the flexible budget (Column 3).

Column 4 contains sales volume variances. Sales volume variances are the differences between the flexible budget (Column 3) and the static budget (Column 5).

See Exhibit 21-4 in your text for an income statement performance report.

A standard cost is a predetermined cost that management expects to attain. Standard cost systems can be used to measure performance, prepare budgets, standardize product costs, and save bookkeeping costs. Variances between actual and standard costs are separated into price variances and efficiency variances for direct materials and direct labor.

OBJECTIVE 3 - COMPUTE DIRECT MATERIALS COST VARIANCES.

The total flexible budget variance for direct materials is separated into the price variance and the efficiency variance. The direct materials price variance measures the difference between the actual and the budgeted price of materials for the amount of materials used.

PRICE VARIANCE = [DIFFERENCE BETWEEN ACTUAL AND BUDGETED UNIT PRICES OF INPUTS] X ACTUAL INPUTS USED

If the actual unit price is less than the budgeted unit price, the variance is favorable. If the actual unit price is greater than the budgeted unit price, the variance is unfavorable.

EFFICIENCY VARIANCE = [INPUTS ACTUALLY USED - INPUTS THAT SHOULD HAVE BEEN USED FOR ACTUAL OUTPUT] X STANDARD UNIT PRICE OF INPUT

The direct materials efficiency (quantity or usage) variance measures the difference between the quantity of inputs actually used and the inputs that should have been used for the actual output achieved.

Note that INPUTS THAT SHOULD HAVE BEEN USED FOR ACTUAL OUTPUT is equal to standard input per unit times actual units produced.

If inputs actually used are less than inputs that should have been used, the variance is favorable. If inputs actually used are greater than inputs that should have been used, the variance is unfavorable.

Exhibit 21-6 in your text summarizes the direct materials variance computations.

OBJECTIVE 4 - COMPUTE DIRECT LABOR COST VARIANCES.

The direct labor price (rate) variance measures the difference between the actual rate per labor hour and the budgeted rate per labor hour.

$$\text{PRICE VARIANCE} = \left[\begin{array}{c}\text{DIFFERENCE BETWEEN}\\ \text{ACTUAL AND BUDGETED}\\ \text{UNIT PRICES OF INPUTS}\end{array}\right] \times \text{ACTUAL INPUTS USED}$$

The direct labor efficiency variance measures the difference between hours actually used and hours that should have been used for the output achieved.

$$\begin{array}{c}\text{EFFICIENCY}\\ \text{VARIANCE}\end{array} = \left[\begin{array}{c}\text{INPUTS}\\ \text{ACTUALLY}\\ \text{USED}\end{array} - \begin{array}{c}\text{INPUTS THAT SHOULD}\\ \text{HAVE BEEN USED}\\ \text{FOR ACTUAL OUTPUT}\end{array}\right] \times \begin{array}{c}\text{STANDARD}\\ \text{UNIT PRICE}\\ \text{OF INPUT}\end{array}$$

Note that these equations are identical to the direct materials variance equations. Exhibit 21-7 in your text summarizes direct labor variance computations.

OBJECTIVE 5 - COMPUTE PRODUCTION OVERHEAD COST VARIANCES.

Overhead variances are computed differently from material and labor variances. This is because overhead has both fixed and variable components. Many companies use a two-variance overhead analysis method. Production overhead variances are commonly separated into a <u>flexible budget variance</u> and a <u>production volume variance</u>.

The total production overhead cost variance is the difference between total actual overhead cost and standard overhead applied to production. The <u>flexible budget production overhead variance</u> is the difference between total actual overhead and the flexible budget amount for actual production volume. The <u>production volume overhead variance</u> is the difference between the flexible budget for actual production and standard overhead applied to production. Exhibit 21-10 in your text summarizes the production overhead variance computations for a two-variance analysis.

Other companies perform a three-variance overhead analysis. This method of analysis splits the <u>flexible budget variance</u> found in a two-variance analysis into a <u>production overhead efficiency variance</u> and a <u>production overhead spending variance</u>.

The <u>production overhead efficiency variance</u> is the difference between the flexible budget for actual production and the flexible budget for actual units of the overhead application base.

The <u>production overhead spending variance</u> is the difference between the flexible budget for actual units of the overhead application base and the total actual overhead cost. Exhibit 21-12 in your text summarizes the production overhead variance computations for a three-variance analysis.

OBJECTIVE 6 - RECORD TRANSACTIONS AT STANDARD COST.

To record direct materials used in production:

Work in Process Inventory (standard cost)	XX	
Direct Materials Efficiency Variance	?*	?*
Direct Materials Price Variance	?*	?*
Materials Inventory (actual cost)		XX

To record direct labor costs:

Work in Process Inventory (standard cost)	XX	
Direct Labor Efficiency Variance	?*	?*
Direct Labor Price Variance	?*	?*
Production Wages (actual cost)		XX

To record production overhead costs:

Work in Process Inventory (standard cost)	XX	
Prod. Overhead Flexible Budget Variance	?*	?*
Prod. Overhead Volume Variance	?*	?*
Production Overhead (actual cost)		XX

* These amounts will be debits if the variances are unfavorable or credits if the variances are favorable.

OBJECTIVE 7 - PREPARE A STANDARD COST INCOME STATEMENT FOR MANAGEMENT.

Some companies record standard cost entries to their accounts. Typically, Work in Process is debited for the standard cost amount, unfavorable variances are debited to variance accounts, favorable variances are credited to variance accounts, and wages and materials are credited to their respective accounts at **actual cost.** A debit balance in a variance account is treated as an expense, while a credit balance is treated as a reduction in expense. The variance accounts are closed to Income Summary.

Exhibit 21-13 in your text illustrates a standard cost income statement. Note that this statement provides a summary of all the variances on the income statement. Tracking variances shows management what needs to be improved or corrected.

TEST YOURSELF

All the self-testing materials in this chapter focus on information and procedures that your instructor is likely to test in quizzes and examinations.

I. MATCHING - MATCH EACH NUMBERED TERM WITH ITS LETTERED DEFINITION.

____ 1. price variance	____ 7. quantity variance
____ 2. standard cost	____ 8. sales volume variance
____ 3. standard cost system	____ 9. static budget
____ 4. variance	____10. flexible budget
____ 5. budget formula	____11. flexible budget variance
____ 6. production volume overhead variance	____12. flexible budget overhead variance

A. A budget prepared for only one level of activity

B. Designed to control costs by analyzing the relationship between actual costs and standard costs

C. Difference between an actual amount and the corresponding budget amount

D. Difference between an amount in the flexible budget and the actual results

E. Difference between a revenue, expense, or operating income in the flexible budget, and the revenue, expense, or income amount in the master budget

F. Difference between total actual overhead (fixed and variable) and the flexible budget amount for actual production volume

G. Difference between the actual unit price of an input (materials and labor) and a standard unit price, multiplied by the actual quantity of inputs used

H. Difference between the flexible budget for actual production and standard overhead applied to production

I. Predetermined cost that management believes the business should incur in producing an item

J. Set of budgets covering a range of volume rather than a single level of volume

K. Shows how to compute the budget amounts

L. Another name for the efficiency variance

II. MULTIPLE CHOICE - CIRCLE THE CORRECT ANSWER.

1. As volume decreases, which of the following is true?

   A. total variable costs decrease
   B. variable cost per unit decreases
   C. fixed cost per unit decreases
   D. total fixed costs increase

2. A budget covering a range of activity levels is a:

   A. flexible budget
   B. static budget
   C. conversion budget
   D. pliable budget

3. Flexible budgets can be used as:

   A. a planning tool
   B. a control device
   C. both a planning tool and a control device
   D. neither a planning tool nor a control device

4. One possible explanation for a favorable sales volume variance and an unfavorable flexible budget variance is:

   A. higher than expected sales and costs
   B. higher than expected sales and lower than expected costs
   C. lower than expected sales and higher than expected costs
   D. lower than expected sales and costs

5. The term standard cost usually refers to _____ cost. The term budgeted cost usually refers to _____ cost.

   A. unit, unit
   B. unit, total
   C. total, unit
   D. total, total

III. COMPLETION - COMPLETE EACH OF THE FOLLOWING STATEMENTS.

1. ____________________ are resources given up to achieve a specific objective.

2. Total ____________________ costs change proportionately with changes in volume or activity.

3. Total ____________________ costs do not change during a given time period over a wide range of volume.

4. A ____________________ cost has both variable and fixed components.

5. If rent expense is fixed at $1,000 per month and sales increase from 2,500 units to 10,000 units, the rent per unit is ____________________ as much as it originally was.

6. A(n) ____________________ variance for materials or labor measures whether the quantity of inputs used to make a product is within the budget.

7. A(n) ____________________ variance for materials or labor measures how well a business keeps unit prices of materials and labor within standards.

IV. EXERCISES

1. Total expenses at a 10,000 unit level are $100,000.

   Total expenses at a 12,000 unit level are $115,000.

   The relevant range is from 3,000 to 20,000 units.

   A. How much are variable costs per unit?

   B. How much are total fixed costs?

   C. What is the flexible budget formula?

   D. At the 4,000 unit level, what are total budgeted expenses?

2. | | |
|---|---|
| Actual production | 3,300 units |
| Actual cost (6,700 feet) | $33,701 |
| Standard price | $4.75 per foot |
| Materials efficiency variance | $2,660 F |

A. Compute the materials price variance.

B. Compute standard feet per unit.

3. 1,900 hours were worked at a rate of $10.50 per hour. The standard rate was $10.00 per hour. 1,850 hours were budgeted for actual output.

A. Compute the labor rate variance.

B. Compute the labor efficiency variance.

4. | | |
|---|---|
| Total actual overhead cost | $26,500 |
| Total flexible budget overhead for actual production | $25,000 |
| Standard overhead applied to production | $25,750 |

A. Compute the flexible budget overhead variance.

B. Compute the production volume variance.

5. Based on a master budget of 22,500 units per month, standard costs are:

Direct materials	$2.40
Direct labor	3.00
Overhead	.75
Standard units cost	$6.15

The flexible overhead budget is:

	Monthly Volume		
Number of units	20,000	30,000	40,000
Standard direct labor hours	1,500	2,250	3,000
Budgeted overhead cost:			
Variable	$6,000	$9,000	$12,000
Fixed	16,875	16,875	16,875

Actual monthly production was 32,000 units. Actual overhead cost was variable, $11,025; and fixed, $16,000. Actual direct labor hours worked was 1990.

A. Compute the total production overhead cost variance.

B. Compute the flexible budget variance.

C. Compute the production volume variance for overhead cost.

D. Compute the production overhead efficiency variance and the production overhead spending variance.

SOLUTIONS

I. MATCHING

1. G 2. I 3. B 4. C 5. K 6. H 7. L 8. E 9. A 10. J
11. D 12. F

II. MULTIPLE CHOICE

1. A Variable costs on a per unit basis are not affected by changes in volume (B). Fixed cost per unit increases as volume decreases (C). Fixed costs do not change as a result of volume changes in the relevant range of production (D).

2. A A static budget is prepared for only one level of activity (B). Answers C and D have no meaning.

3. C All budgets are used for planning. Since the flexible budget is prepared for the actual level of activity achieved, it provides for precise control.

4. A The sales volume variance measures differences between the static budget and the flexible budget for actual volume achieved. The flexible budget variance measures differences between actual results and the flexible budget for actual volume achieved. Accordingly, higher than expected sales could be expected to give a favorable sales volume variance, and actual costs above flexible budget costs could be expected to give an unfavorable flexible budget variance.

5. B A standard cost is a carefully predetermined cost that is usually expressed on a per-unit basis. It is a target cost, a cost that should be attained. Budgeted costs are total costs. Think of a standard variable cost as a budget for a single unit.

III. COMPLETION

1. costs
2. variable
3. fixed
4. mixed
5. one-fourth (2,500 units / 10,000 units)
6. efficiency
7. price

IV. EXERCISES

1. A. ($115,000 - $100,000) / (12,000 - 10,000) = $7.50

   B. 10,000 units X $7.50 + Fixed Costs = $100,000
   $75,000 + Fixed Costs = $100,000
   Fixed Costs = $ 25,000

   C. Total Budgeted Costs = $7.50 X number of units produced + $25,000

   D. Total budgeted costs = $7.50 X 4,000 + $25,000 = $55,000

2. A.

Actual cost	$33,701	
Less: Budgeted unit cost X actual usage		
$4.75 X 6,700	31,825	
Material price variance	$ 1,876	U

B. $2,660 F = (6,700 feet - X) X $4.75
X = 7,260 feet = inputs that should have been used
7,260 feet ÷ 3,300 units = 2.2 standard feet

3. A.

Actual costs (1,900 hours X $10.50)	$19,950	
Budgeted costs for actual labor hours		
(1,900 hours X $10.00)	19,000	
Labor rate variance	$ 950	U

B.

Budgeted costs for actual labor hours		
(1,900 hours X $10.00)	$19,000	
Standard cost for actual production		
(1,850 hours X $10.00)	18,500	
Labor efficiency variance	$ 500	U

4. A.

Total actual overhead	$26,500	
Total flexible budget overhead for		
actual production	25,000	
Flexible overhead budget variance	$ 1,500	U

B.

Standard overhead applied to production	$25,750	
Total flexible budget overhead for		
actual production	25,000	
Production volume variance	$ 750	F

5. A.

Variable overhead	$11,025	
Fixed overhead	16,000	
Total actual overhead cost		$27,075
Standard overhead applied to production		
32,000 units X $0.75		24,000
Total production overhead cost variance		$ 3,075

B.

Variable overhead	$11,025	
Fixed overhead	16,000	
Total actual overhead cost		$27,075
Variable overhead 32,000 units X .075 DLH X $4	$ 9,600	
Fixed overhead	16,875	
Flexible budget for actual production		$26,475
Flexible budget variance		$ 600 U

C.	Flexible budget for actual production	
	Variable overhead 32,000 units X .075 DLH X $4	$ 9,600
	Fixed overhead	16,875
		$26,475
	Standard overhead applied to production	
	32,000 units X $0.75	24,000
	Production volume overhead variance	$ 2,475 U

D.	Flexible budget for actual production	$26,475
	Flexible budget for actual DLH	
	1990 DLH X $4[1] + $16,875	24,835
	Production overhead efficiency variance	$ 1,640 U

[1] Variable cost per DLH = Variable overhead / Std DLH

= $6,000 / 1,500 Std DLH

= $4 per direct labor hour

Flexible budget for actual DLH	$24,835
Total actual overhead cost	27,075
Production overhead spending variance	$ 2,240 F

DEMONSTRATION PROBLEM 1

Part A - Income statement performance report.

A flexible budget for Strawser's Straw Hat Co. is presented below:

Strawser's Straw Hat Co.
Flexible Budget
For the Year January - December, 19X9

	Budget Formula per unit	Various Levels of Volume		
Units	-	20,000	24,000	28,000
Sales	$9.50	$190,000	$228,000	$266,000
Variable expenses	4.40	88,000	105,600	123,200
Fixed expenses	-	54,000	54,000	54,000
Total expenses		142,000	159,600	177,200
Operating income		$ 48,000	$ 68,400	$ 88,800

The static (master) budget is based on volume of 24,000 hats. Actual operating results for 19X9 are as follows:

Sales (25,500 hats)	$235,875
Variable expenses	109,825
Fixed expenses	57,570

REQUIRED:

1. Prepare an income statement performance report for 19X9.

2. Show that the total net variances in operating income account for the net difference between actual operating income and the static (master) budget income.

Part A

Requirement 1 - Income statement performance report.

Strawser's Straw Hat Co.
Income Statement Performance Report
For the Year Ended December 31, 19X9

	(1) Actual Results at Actual Prices	(2) (1) - (3) Flexible Budget Variances	(3) Flexible Budget for Actual Volume Achieved	(4) (3) - (5) Sales Volume Variances	(5) Static (Master) Budget
Units	______	______	______	______	______
Sales	$______	$______	$______	$______	$______
Variable expenses					
Fixed expenses	______	______	______	______	______
Total expenses	______	______	______	______	______
Operating income	$______	$______	$______	$______	$______

Requirement 2 (reconciling variances)

$

______

$______

$

______

$______

DEMONSTRATION PROBLEM 2

Part B - Direct material and direct labor variances.

Presented below are standard cost facts pertinent to the production of Strawser's Straw Hat Co. for 19X9:

Strawser's Straw Hat Co.
Standard Cost Facts
For the Year January - December, 19X9

Panel A - Comparison of Actual Results with Flexible Budget.
Sold 25,500 straw hats.

	Actual Results at Actual Prices	Flexible Budget	Flexible Budget Variances
Variable expenses:			
Direct materials	$ 17,030	$ 17,850	$ 820 F
Direct labor	46,620	45,900	720 U
Variable production overhead	23,700	25,500	1,800 F
Selling and administrative expenses	22,475	22,950	475 F
Total variable expenses	109,825	112,200	2,375 F
Fixed expenses:			
Fixed production overhead	34,900	36,000	1,100 F
Selling and administrative expenses	22,670	18,000	4,670 U
Total fixed expenses	57,570	54,000	3,570 U
Total expenses	$167,395	$166,200	$1,195 U

Panel B - Standards for Direct Material and Direct Labor Flexible Budget:
25,500 straw hats.

	(1) Standard Inputs Budgeted for 25,500 hats	(2) Standard Price per Unit of Input	(1) x (2) Flexible Budget for 25,500 Finished Units of Output
Direct materials	1 pound x 25,500	$ .70	$17,850
Direct labor	1/4 hour x 25,500	7.20	45,900

Strawser's Straw Hat Co.
Flexible Production Overhead Cost Budget

	(Actual)	(Static) (Budget)
Number of hats sold	25,500	24,000
Standard direct labor hours	6,375	6,000
Budgeted production overhead cost:		
Variable	$25,500	$24,000
Fixed	36,000	36,000
Total	$61,500	$60,000

Overhead rates per direct labor hour:

Standard variable overhead rate ($24,000 ÷ 6,000 hours)	=	$ 4.00
Standard fixed overhead rate ($36,000 ÷ 6,000 hours)	=	$ 6.00
Standard total overhead rate ($60,000 ÷ 6,000 hours)	=	$10.00

Actual direct material and direct labor expenses for the year are:

Direct materials	26,200 pounds @ $.65 per pound
Direct labor	6,300 hours @ $7.40 per hour

REQUIRED:

1. Compute the direct materials and direct labor price and efficiency variances.

2. Compute the total variance, the flexible budget variance, and the production volume variance for overhead. (Ignore selling and administrative expenses.)

3. Prepare an income statement through operating income. Report all production cost variances. Use actual sales revenue of $235,875 from Part A.

Requirement 1

Price Variances

Direct materials price variance

Direct labor price variance

Efficiency Variances

Direct materials efficiency variance

Direct labor efficiency variance

Requirement 2 (overhead variances)

Total overhead variance:

$

$ ______

Flexible budget variance:

$

$ ______

Production volume variance:

$

$ ______

Requirement 3

Strawser's Straw Hat Co.
Income Statement
For the Month Ended March 31, 19X4

Sales				$
Cost of goods sold at standard cost			$	
Cost variances:	Favorable	Unfavorable		
Direct materials price	$	$		
Direct materials efficiency				
Direct labor price				
Direct labor efficiency				
Overhead flexible budget				
Overhead production volume				
	$	$		
Net cost variance			$	
Cost of goods sold at actual cost				
Gross profit				
Selling and administrative				
Operating income				$

22

Responsibility Accounting

CHAPTER REVIEW

Responsibility accounting is a system used to evaluate the performance of managers based on the activities they supervise.

A responsibility center can be any subunit of an organization which management wishes to evaluate. Three common types of responsibility centers are: (1) cost centers, (2) profit centers, and (3) investment centers.

OBJECTIVE 1 - IDENTIFY DIFFERENT TYPES OF RESPONSIBILITY CENTERS, AND SPECIFY THE INFORMATION THEY REPORT.

A cost center generates no revenue and is evaluated on cost control.

A profit center such as a sales department is evaluated on its revenues, expenses, and income profit.

An investment center such as a single department store in a chain is evaluated on its revenues, expenses, income, and investment needed to finance its operations.

OBJECTIVE 2 - PREPARE A PERFORMANCE REPORT FOR MANAGEMENT BY EXCEPTION.

Management by exception is a strategy in which management investigates important deviations from budgeted amounts. Responsibility and authority are delegated to lower-level employees; management does not become involved unless necessary. Exhibit 22-2 in your text illustrates a performance report which stresses variances. The format of a performance report is a matter of personal preference of the users. Basically, the report compares actual and budgeted performance at different levels of the organization.

OBJECTIVE 3 - ALLOCATE INDIRECT COSTS TO DEPARTMENTS.

The most common responsibility center is a department. Operating departments add value to products or services sold to customers. Service departments provide services to operating departments and other service departments. Calculating departmental costs and operating income can be difficult because of indirect costs. Direct costs can be traced to a department, but indirect costs are not traceable to a single department.

Cost allocations assign various indirect costs to departments. An allocation base is a logical common denominator used to assign a specific cost to two or more departments. For example, heating cost allocation may be based on a department's cubic footage. Exhibit 22-3 lists typical allocation bases for various types of costs.

The general method to allocate costs is:

(1) Determine the allocation base.

(2) Obtain the proportion of the allocation base assigned to each department.

(3) Multiply the cost by the proportion assigned to each department to obtain the cost assigned to each department.

The direct method of service department cost allocation ignores all service department costs provided to other service departments. All service department costs are allocated directly to production departments. Exhibit 22-5 in your text illustrates the direct method of cost allocation.

The step-down method of cost allocation recognizes in part the cost of services provided by service departments to other service departments. The order of allocating service department costs affects the amounts ultimately allocated to production departments. Exhibit 22-6 in your text illustrates the step-down method of cost allocation.

OBJECTIVE 4 - PREPARE A DEPARTMENTAL INCOME STATEMENT.

Exhibit 22-7 in your text illustrates a departmental income statement.

Some companies prepare departmental income statements that emphasize the difference between direct departmental expenses and indirect expenses allocated from other departments. Once indirect costs are allocated, a departmental income statement may be prepared using this format:

Net sales	$XXX
Cost of goods sold	XXX
Gross margin	XXX
Various operating expenses	XXX
Margin before indirect expenses	XXX
Indirect expenses	XXX
Operating income	$XXX

OBJECTIVE 5 - ACCOUNT FOR BRANCH OPERATIONS.

Many companies have operations in multiple locations. The main location is usually the home office, while all other locations are branches. Branch accounting is a system that separates the accounts of a branch from those of the home office.

Reciprocal accounts are accounts that have exactly offsetting balances and are used to control a general ledger that is kept in two or more locations.

The home office maintains a reciprocal account entitled Branch-Factory Ledger Control. This account can be viewed as an investment in the branch or a receivable from the branch.

The branch maintains a reciprocal account entitled Home-Office Ledger Control. This account can be viewed as owner equity of the home office or a payable to the home office.

Carefully study Exhibit 22-8 in your text showing sample journal entries for branch accounting. Notice that when the home office incurs branch-related obligations such as accounts payable or wages payable, it debits Branch-Factory

Ledger Control and credits the regular general ledger account. When the branch records these items, it debits regular general ledger accounts such as Direct Materials Inventory and Factory Wages, and credits Home-Office Ledger Control.

Branch accounting may be instituted for sales branches and international operations.

TEST YOURSELF

All the self-testing materials in this chapter focus on information and procedures that your instructor is likely to test in quizzes and examinations.

I. MATCHING - MATCH EACH NUMBERED TERM WITH ITS LETTERED DEFINITION.

____ 1. allocation base

____ 2. branch ledger

____ 3. direct expense

____ 4. factory ledger

____ 5. indirect expense

____ 6. reciprocal accounts

____ 7. responsibility accounting

____ 8. branch accounting

____ 9. cost allocation

____10. expense allocation

____11. home-office ledger

____12. management by exception

____13. responsibility center

A. A branch ledger for a manufacturing plant

B. A system for separating the accounts of a branch of a business from the accounts of the home office

C. Any subunit of an organization needing control

D. Assignment of various expenses to the departments of a business

E. Assignment of various costs to the departments of a business

F. Expense that is conveniently identified with, and traceable to, a particular department of a business

G. Expenses that are not conveniently traceable to a single department

H. Logical common denominator for assigning a given cost to two or more departments of a business

I. Management strategy in which executive attention is directed to the important deviations from budgeted amounts

J. System for evaluating the progress of managers based on activities under their supervision

K. The part of a general ledger kept by a branch of a business

L. The part of a general ledger kept by the home office

M. Two or more accounts that have the same offsetting balances and are used to control a general ledger that is kept in two or more locations

II. MULTIPLE CHOICE - CIRCLE THE CORRECT ANSWER.

1. An example of a profit center is:

   A. housewares department in a department store
   B. product line in a hardware store
   C. both of these
   D. neither of these

2. An example of an investment center is:

   A. a department store in a chain of stores
   B. the delivery department of an auto parts store
   C. the shipping department of a manufacturer
   D. both B and C

3. Which factor is important in an effective responsibility accounting system?

   A. control over operations
   B. access to information
   C. both of these
   D. neither of these

4. Responsibility accounting systems are used for:

   A. finding fault
   B. placing blame
   C. both finding fault and placing blame
   D. determining who can explain specific variances

5. Indirect expenses are:

   A. all costs other than direct expenses
   B. traceable to a single department
   C. costs which cannot be allocated
   D. direct material and direct labor

6. The most logical way of allocating payroll department costs would be:

   A. square feet of space
   B. cubic feet of space
   C. number of orders in each department
   D. number of employees in each department

7. The most logical way of allocating janitorial services would be:

   A. by square feet of space
   B. in proportion to newspaper advertising space
   C. by number of orders in each department
   D. by number of employees in each department

8. Which of the following would be unlikely to appear in a branch ledger for a manufacturing firm?

   A. Branch Ledger Control
   B. Direct Materials Inventory
   C. Home-Office Ledger Control
   D. Work in Process Inventory

9. When materials are used by a branch, the entry in the home office journal would:

   A. debit Work in Process Inventory
   B. debit Branch Ledger Control
   C. credit Direct Materials Inventory
   D. not be made

10. When wages are recorded and payable by the home office on behalf of the branch, the entry in the branch factory journal would:

   A. credit Factory Wages
   B. credit Home-Office Ledger Control
   C. credit Wages Payable
   D. debit Branch Ledger Control

III. COMPLETION - COMPLETE EACH OF THE FOLLOWING STATEMENTS.

1. The basic unit in a responsibility accounting system is called a

   ______________________________.

2. A(n) ____________ center is responsible for controlling costs.

3. A(n) ____________ center reports revenues, expenses, and income.

4. A(n) ____________ center reports revenues, expenses, income, and the investment needed to finance operations.

5. A personnel department and a shipping department are examples of

   ______________________________ centers.

6. ______________________ directs executive attention to important deviations from budgeted amounts.

7. A logical common denominator for assigning a given cost to two or more departments is an ______________________.

8. ____________________ are two or more accounts that have the same offsetting balances and are used to control a general ledger that is kept in two or more locations.

9. When shipments of finished goods are transferred from the factory to the home-office managed warehouses, the ______________________ account will be credited in the ____________________ and the ______________________ account will be debited in the ______________________________.

IV. EXERCISES

1. Bocock Corp. operates sales offices across the United States. The following transactions were completed during May:

   1) Sold merchandise for cash, $5,000.
   2) Transferred $4,000 cash to the home office.
   3) The home office paid commission on the $5,000 sale, $500.
   4) The branch paid the telephone bill, $250.

   A. Record the appropriate entries for the home office.

   B. Record the appropriate entries for the branch office.

2. Simpson's Department Store sells family clothing. Monthly rent is $60,000. The following data is available for January, 19X6:

Department	Sales	Square Feet Occupied
Men's	$210,000	11,000
Women's	294,000	15,000
Children's	106,000	4,000

A. Allocate rent to each department based on sales.

B. Allocate rent to each department based on square feet occupied.

SOLUTIONS

I. MATCHING

1. H 2. K 3. F 4. A 5. G 6. M 7. J 8. B 9. E 10. D
11. L 12. I 13. C

II. MULTIPLE CHOICE

1. A 2. A 3. C 4. D 5. A 6. D 7. A 8. A 9. B 10. B

III. COMPLETION

1. responsibility center
2. cost
3. profit
4. investment
5. cost
6. Management by exception
7. allocation base
8. Reciprocal accounts
9. Branch Ledger Control
   home-office journal
   Home-Office Ledger Control
   branch factory journal

IV. EXERCISES

1.

A. 1)	Branch Ledger Control	5,000	
	Sales Revenue		5,000
2)	Cash	4,000	
	Branch Ledger Control		4,000
3)	Sales Commission Expense	500	
	Cash		500
4)	Utility Expense	250	
	Branch Ledger Control		250
B. 1)	Cash	5,000	
	Home-Office Ledger Control		5,000
2)	Home-Office Ledger Control	4,000	
	Cash		4,000
3)	no entry is required		
4)	Home-Office Ledger Control	250	
	Cash		250

2.

A. Allocation based on sales:

Total sales = $210,000 + $294,000 + $106,000 = $600,000

Men's department rent = ($210,000 ÷ $600,000) X $60,000 = $21,000
Women's department rent = ($294,000 ÷ $600,000) X $60,000 = $29,400
Children's department rent = ($106,000 ÷ $600,000) X $60,000 = $10,600

Total rent allocated = $21,000 + $29,400 + $10,600 = $60,000

B. Allocation based on square feet occupied:

Total square feet occupied = 11,000 + 15,000 + 4,000 = 30,000

Men's department rent = (11,000 ÷ 30,000) X $60,000 = $22,000
Women's department rent = (15,000 ÷ 30,000) X $60,000 = $30,000
Children's department rent = (4,000 ÷ 30,000) X $60,000 = $ 8,000

Total rent allocated = $22,000 + $30,000 + $ 8,000 = $60,000

DEMONSTRATION PROBLEM 1: Allocation of Expense

Chaux's clothing store sells women's clothing in 4,000 square feet of space, men's clothing in 4,400 square feet of space, and children's clothing in 6,000 square feet of space. The entire store has 15,000 square feet and the monthly rent is $60,000. The location of the women's department is twice as valuable as the men's department, which is considered average. The location of the children's department is considered 60% as valuable per square foot as the men's department.

REQUIRED:

Prepare an analysis to show how much total rent expense should be allocated to each department, and determine each department's rent expense per square foot.

DEMONSTRATION PROBLEM 2: Home-Office and Branch Journals

Baked Alaska, Inc., has organized its manufacturing operations as branches. The home office is in Juneau, and branches are located throughout the southern states. The home office makes all purchases and sales, handles cash payments and cash receipts, incurs all liabilities, and controls the central warehouses in which the frozen confections are stored after the finished goods are transferred from the branches. During a recent month, the following transactions were completed:

A. Direct materials for a branch were purchased on account $4,000
B. Direct materials used by the branch in production, $3,600
C. Branch payroll paid, $7,900
D. Branch overhead applied, $3,950
E. Goods shipped to central warehouse, $14,400
F. Sales on account, $20,000 (cost of sales, $6,000)
G. Collections on account, $17,800

REQUIRED:

Journalize these transactions for the home office and the branch.

GENERAL JOURNAL - HOME OFFICE

Entry	Account and Explanation	PR	Debit	Credit

Strategy, Cost Management And Continuous Improvement

CHAPTER REVIEW

OBJECTIVE 1 - DESCRIBE THE DISTINCTIVE FEATURES OF ACTIVITY-BASED COSTING (ABC).

Activity-based costing (ABC) focuses on activities and the costs of those activities. Thus, the cost of a product or service is "built up" from the cost of the specific activities undertaken to manufacture or provide it. Refer to Exhibit 23-1 in your text for an overview of the relationships among business functions, departments, and activities.

Activity-based costing has gained popularity because many costs in business are the result of several factors. Contrast this idea with the more traditional accounting practice of allocating all overhead costs to products based on direct labor. Moreover, many activities are not confined to a single department. For example, inspection of products may take place in several departments.

In a manufacturing company, product costs follow the pattern of other costing systems for direct materials. Conversion costs, however, are applied based on the activities that take place, rather than using a single application base.

Finally, ABC provides full cost information, including upstream activities such as product design, and downstream activities such as marketing, distribution, and customer service. Note that full product cost information is used internally, while external financial statements continue to reflect traditional costing practices.

OBJECTIVE 2 - USE ACTIVITY-BASED COSTS TO MAKE MANAGEMENT DECISIONS.

Traditional costing systems consider items such as machinery setup to be overhead. ABC treats setup costs as an activity. Since setup costs can be significant, companies may find that properly identifying these costs and allocating them appropriately results in more precise costing information. Many companies have found that it is not economical to incur large setup costs for small production runs, and in some cases they have found that it is cheaper to buy certain items from outside suppliers rather than continue to manufacture them.

OBJECTIVE 3 - COMPARE THE MAJOR FEATURES OF A JUST-IN-TIME (JIT) PRODUCTION SYSTEM AND A TRADITIONAL SYSTEM.

Traditional systems have produced enormous waste in areas such as inventories and manufacturing processes. Holding large amounts of inventory requires a large investment. Similarly, maintaining large stocks of raw materials and finished goods to protect against poor quality and machine breakdowns also costs money.

Just-in-time (JIT) systems are designed to eliminate waste. JIT arranges production activity so that production moves continuously from production process to production process. Factories are arranged so that machinery is located according to the step in the production process instead of according to the type of machine. JIT also focuseS on reducing setup times, so as to keep the flow of production moving.

Another focus of JIT is to schedule production so as to produce only what is needed to meet sales demand. This allows companies to reduce inventory investment. Manufacturing is activated by customer orders. The final activity in the manufacturing process "pulls" the needed quantities from the previous process. Finally, suppliers are expected to deliver frequent quantities of defect-free raw material.

OBJECTIVE 4 - RECORD MANUFACTURING COSTS FOR A BACKFLUSH COSTING SYSTEM.

Two characteristics of backflush costing are (1) standard costs for each product, and either low or constant levels of direct materials and work in process.

Backflush costing combines raw material and work in process into a single raw and in process account. The more popular backflush costing systems have two <u>trigger points</u> which result in entries in the accounting records. One is the purchase of direct materials, and the other is the completion of finished goods. Review this section in your text to familiarize yourself with these entries and the entries for variances.

OBJECTIVE 5 - PREPARE A LIFE-CYCLE BUDGET FOR A PRODUCT.

The life-cycle budget is prepared for the entire estimated life of a product. The general format of a life-cycle budget is:

Sales
- Direct materials and purchased parts
= Material contribution margin
- Variable conversion costs
= Variable conversion cost contribution margin
- Fixed conversion costs
= Product manufacturing contribution
- Other fixed costs
= Life-cycle operating contribution

OBJECTIVE 6 - RELATE TARGET COSTING AND KAIZEN COSTING TO CONTINUOUS IMPROVEMENT.

Target costing is a cost management technique whereby managers set goals for cost reduction through product design. Kaizen is a Japanese word for continuous improvement. The objectives of such systems is to reduce costs by improving efficiency while maintaining quality.

OBJECTIVE 7 - CONTRAST THE FOUR TYPES OF QUALITY COSTS.

<u>Total quality management</u> is an effort to improve quality throughout an organization. Certain costs are incurred in the effort to achieve quality products and services.

<u>Prevention costs</u> are incurred to avoid producing poor-quality goods or services.

Appraisal costs are incurred to detect poor-quality goods or services during the production process. Internal failure costs are incurred to fix flaws before delivery to the customer. External failure costs are incurred to fix flaws that are detected after delivery to the customer. Refer to exhibit 23-6 in your text for examples of costs of quality.

TEST YOURSELF

All the self-testing materials in this chapter focus on information and procedures that your instructor is likely to test in quizzes and examinations.

I. MATCHING - MATCH EACH NUMBERED TERM WITH ITS LETTERED DEFINITION.

____ 1. activity-based costing

____ 2. product life cycle

____ 3. backflush costing

____ 4. total quality management

____ 5. external failure costs

____ 6. just-in-time (JIT)

____ 7. Kaizen costing

____ 8. appraisal costs

____ 9. benchmarking

____10. internal failure costs

____11. activity-based management (ABM)

____12. life-cycle budget

____13. non-value-added activities

____14. prevention costs

____15. quality

____16. strategy

____17. target costing

____18. throughput time

____19. trigger points

____20. value engineering

A. a formal effort to improve quality throughout an organization's value chain

B. the time from original research and development to the end of a product's sales and customer servicing

C. a system that focuses on activities as the fundamental cost objects and uses the costs of those activities as the building blocks for compiling the costs of products and other cost objects

D. production systems designed to eliminate waste by such means as sequentially arranged production activities, low setup times, demand-pull production scheduling, and a high level of employee training and commitment

E. the relentless pursuit of cost reduction in the manufacturing stage of a product's life cycle, achieved by planned reductions in cost drivers

F. costs incurred when poor-quality goods or services are detected after delivery to customers

G. a standard costing system that starts with output completed and works backward to apply manufacturing costs to units sold and inventories.

H. a set of business goals and the tactics to achieve them

I. a management process that focuses on the management of activities as the way to improve value received by customers

J. a cost management technique that helps managers set goals for cost reductions through product design

K. a budget that compiles predicted revenues and costs of a product over its entire life cycle

L. activities that do not increase customer value or satisfy a company need

M. comparison of current performance with some standard

N. costs incurred to avoid poor-quality goods or services

O. costs incurred when poor-quality goods or services are detected before delivery to customers

P. costs incurred in detecting poor-quality goods or services

Q. design activities aimed at achieving cost targets while designing high-quality, high-performance products that satisfy the customer

R. points in the operations that prompt entries in the accounting records

S. the conformance of the attributes of a product or service with a specific set of standards

T. the time between receipt of purchased materials and completion of finished products

II. MULTIPLE CHOICE - CIRCLE THE CORRECT ANSWER.

1. Which of the following is a value-added activity?

   A. processing time
   B. waiting time
   C. moving time
   D. reworking time

2. Which of the following is not an internal failure cost?

   A. rework
   B. rejected product units
   C. warranty costs
   D. scrap

3. Which of the following is an external failure cost?

   A. warranty costs
   B. rework
   C. inspection
   D. preventive maintenance

4. In activity-based costing, cost allocations are made based on

   A. direct labor hours
   B. machine hours
   C. several different cost drivers
   D. direct labor cost

5. Which of the following is not a characteristic or goal of just-in-time systems?

   A. elimination of waste
   B. maintaining high levels of inventory
   C. reducing setup times
   D. production levels based on customer demand

6. In a just-in-time production system, manufacturing activity is usually initiated by

   A. the production manager
   B. receipt of an order from a customer
   C. decreases in inventory levels
   D. the president of the company

7. Which costing approach focuses cost-reduction efforts on the design stage of a product?

   A. activity-based costing
   B. kaizen costing
   C. just-in-time
   D. target costing

III. COMPLETION - COMPLETE EACH OF THE FOLLOWING STATEMENTS.

1. A just-in-time production system is designed to eliminate ______________________________.

2. Full product cost includes ______________________________, ______________________________, and ______________________________.

3. Training of company personnel is an example of ________________________.

4. A backflush costing system merges the direct materials and work in process accounts into a ____ account.

5. A product life cycle is the time from ______________________________ to ______________________________.

6. ______________________________ refers to design activities aimed at achieving cost targets while designing high-quality, high-performance products that satisfy the customer.

7. Four types of quality costs are ____________________, ____________________, ____________________, and ____________________.

IV. EXERCISES

1. Yellow Dawn uses activity-based costing to account for its manufacturing process. The company has 4 activities: material handling, equipment setup, batching of raw materials, and packaging. The budgeted costs for 19X6 and their cost drivers are as follows:

Activity	Total Budgeted Cost	Cost Driver
Materials handling	$ 38,400	Number of pallets moved
Equipment setup	3,825	Number of setups
Batching	144,000	Number of batches
Packaging	96,000	Number of bags filled

Dawn expects to produce 32,000 batches of chemicals during the year. Production is expected to involve the movement of 64,000 pallets of materials and 45 setups, and use 64,000,000 bags.

A. Compute the four application rates for activity costs.

B. If a batch of chemicals requires the movement of 3 pallets of raw materials, no setup, batching, and 2200 bags for packaging, compute the average manufacturing cost of the batch (excluding direct materials).

2. Data Disks Manufacturing produces compact disks for computers. Data Disks uses a backflush costing system with two trigger points: the purchase of direct materials and the transfer to finished goods. One of the company's products has a standard direct materials cost of $7.50 per unit and a standard conversion cost of $35 per unit.

During the year Data Disks produced 100,000 units and sold 95,000. It purchased direct materials having a standard cost of $420,000, and incurred actual conversion costs totaling $3,912,500.

A. Prepare summary journal entries for the year.

Date	Account and Explanation	PR	Debit	Credit

B. Assume that the balance in RIP inventory was $450,000. What is the year end balance in RIP inventory?

C. Is conversion cost overapplied or underapplied for the year? By how much?

3. Terrific Toys produces electronic toys. Engineering is developing a new line of laser light swords with an expected life cycle of 3 years. Sales are predicted to be 15,000 units at $16 each over the next 3 years. Given current technology, the swords can be manufactured for the following product-line costs:

Fixed conversion costs	$75,000
Direct materials	4 per unit
Variable conversion costs	2 per unit

A. Prepare an initial life-cycle budget through the product-line manufacturing contribution.

B. At the predicted volume of 15,000 swords, what is the original budgeted cost per unit?

C. What percent of sales revenue is the initial product-line manufacturing contribution?

SOLUTIONS

I. MATCHING

1. C	2. B	3. G	4. A	5. F	6. D	7. E	8. P	9. M	10. O
11. I	12. K	13. L	14. N	15. S	16. H	17. J	18. T	19. R	20. Q

II. MULTIPLE CHOICE

1. A
2. C
3. A
4. C
5. B
6. B
7. D

III. COMPLETION

1. waste
2. upstream activities, total manufacturing costs, upstream activities
3. prevention costs
4. raw and in process
5. original research and development, the end of a product's sales and customer servicing
6. value-engineering
7. prevention, appraisal, internal failure, external failure

IV. EXERCISES

1. A.

Activity	Cost of Activity		Cost Driver Application base		Cost per unit of application base
Materials handling	$38,400	÷	64,000	=	$ .60
Equipment setup	3,825	÷	45	=	85.00
Batching	144,000	÷	32,000	=	4.50
Packaging	96,000	÷	64,000,000	=	.015

B.

Materials handling	3 pallets X	$ .60	$ 1.80
Equipment setup	0 setups X	$85.00	-0-
Batching	1 batching X	$ 4.50	4.50
Packaging	2,200 bags X	$ .015	33.00
Total manufacturing cost for this batch			$39.30

2. A.

RIP Inventory	420,000	
Accounts Payable		420,000
Conversion Costs	3,912,500	
Various Accounts		3,912,500
Finished Goods	4,250,000	
RIP Inventory		750,000
Conversion Costs		3,500,000

Cost of Goods Sold	412,500	
Conversion Costs		412,500

B.

RIP Inventory - beginning balance	$450,000
Additions	420,000
	$870,000
Reductions	750,000
RIP Inventory - ending balance	$120,000

C.

Conversion costs incurred	$3,912,500
Conversion costs applied	3,500,000
Underapplied Conversion costs	$ 412,000

3. A. Initial Life-Cycle Budget
Proposed Laser-light Sword
Predicted Sales Volume, 15,000 Swords

Sales @ $16	$240,000
Direct materials @ $4	60,000
Materials contribution margin	$180,000
Variable conversion costs @ $2	30,000
Variable conversion cost contribution margin	$150,000
Fixed conversion costs	75,000
Product-line manufacturing contribution	$ 75,000

B.

Direct materials	$ 4.00	
Variable conversion costs	2.00	
Fixed conversion costs	5.00	($75,000 / 15,000 swords)
Budgeted cost per unit	$11.00	

C. Product-line manufacturing contribution / Sales revenue

= $75,000 / $240,000 = 31.25 %

DEMONSTRATION PROBLEM 1

Tupelo Turbine Engines, a manufacturing company, uses activity-based costing. A major hydroelectric contractor has asked for a bid on 500 turbine engines that will be installed in future power stations. Tupelo's costing system has the following features:

Activity	Cost Driver	Conversion Cost per unit of the application base
Purchasing	Number of purchase orders	$75.00
Assembly	Number of parts	5.00
Testing	Number of hours of testing	25.00

Each turbine engine has 1280 parts; total direct materials cost $5,000 per engine; and 10 hours of testing. A total of 800 purchase orders will be necessary if the contractor accepts Tupelo's bid.

REQUIRED:

1. Compute the total cost that Tupelo will incur to purchase the needed parts and assemble and test the 500 turbine engines. Also compute the average cost per unit.

2. Assume that, for bidding purposes, Tupelo adds a 30 % markup to total cost. What price will the company bid for the order?

3. Suppose that, instead of an ABC system, Tupelo has a traditional product costing system that applies all conversion costs to products at the plant-wide rate of $31 per direct labor hour. The engine contract will require 100,000 hours. What price will the company bid for the order?

DEMONSTRATION PROBLEM 2

Fogelsong Industries is considering a new product line of table saws. The budgeted average sales price is $1,200. The desired life-cycle manufacturing contribution is $450 per table saw.

REQUIRED:

1. Compute the allowable manufacturing cost per unit.

2. The kaizen cost reduction for the product line's life cycle is expected to be $50 per table saw. The value-engineering cost reduction goal has been set at $120 per table saw. Compute the target cost and the budgeted unit manufacturing cost in the initial life-cycle budget.

3. Some of Fogelsong's costs are:

   a. Rejections at final inspection
   b. Quality awareness training for assembly workers
   c. Inspection of incoming raw materials
   d. Warranty repairs

   Identify each cost as belonging to one of the following categories of quality costs: appraisal, external failure, internal failure, or prevention.

24

Special Business Decisions And Pricing

CHAPTER REVIEW

OBJECTIVE 1 - IDENTIFY THE RELEVANT INFORMATION FOR A SPECIAL BUSINESS DECISION.

Relevant information is expected future information which differs among the alternative courses of action. Information which does not differ is irrelevant and will not change a business decision.

OBJECTIVE 2 - MAKE NINE TYPES OF SPECIAL BUSINESS DECISIONS.

(1) Special sales orders are evaluated by comparing the expected increase in revenues to the expected increase in expenses. If fixed expenses do not change, they are not relevant and should not be considered in the analysis.

A quick summary analysis (Exhibit 24-2 in your text) subtracts the expected increase in expenses from the expected increase in revenues to arrive at the expected increase in operating income. An income statement analysis with and without the special order (Exhibit 24-3) compares total revenues, expenses, and operating income for both courses of action. (Both analyses should give you the same results.)

Several points about special sales orders need to be considered. Will the sale affect regular business? Does the company have the excess capacity to produce the special order?

(2) When considering the deletion of products, departments, or territories, with no change in fixed costs, the only relevant information is the expected decreases in revenues and variable expenses, which together show the contribution margin and change in operating income. Study Exhibit 24-4 in your text.

(3) When considering the deletion of products, departments, or territories with a change in fixed costs, the analysis must include the change in fixed expenses as well as changes in variable expenses and revenues. Refer to Exhibit 24-5 for an example.

(4) When considering which product to emphasize, a company generally will emphasize products with the highest profit margins. Sometimes, a constraint or limiting factor exists. A constraint restricts production or sales. Constraints may be stated in terms of labor hours, machine hours, materials, or storage space.

The way to maximize profits for a given capacity is to maximize the contribution margin per unit of the limiting factor. Exhibit 24-6 in your text presents an example of how to maximize the contribution margin per labor hour.

(5) The make or buy decision determines how best to use available facilities. The relevant information for the make analysis includes: (1) direct materials, (2) direct labor, (3) variable overhead, and (4) fixed overhead. The relevant information for the buy analysis is: (1) the fixed overhead that will continue whether the part is made or bought and (2) the purchase price to buy the part. This analysis shows whether it is cheaper to make the part or to buy the part. Review Exhibit 24-7 in your text.

(6) Sometimes facilities can be used to make other products if the product currently produced is purchased from an outside supplier. In the make or buy decision, the alternatives become: (1) make, (2) buy and leave the facilities idle, and (3) buy and use the facilities for other products. As indicated in Exhibit 24-8, the alternative with the lowest net cost is the best use of the facilities.

(7) The sell as-is or process further decision compares the expected net revenue (revenue minus costs) of processing further with selling inventory as-is. Exhibit 24-9 illustrates the sell as-is or process further decision. Note that past historical costs of inventory are sunk costs--they cannot make a difference to the decision; the sunk costs are irrelevant because they are the same under both alternatives.

(8) The replacement of equipment decision requires the manager to focus on relevant items that differ between alternatives. The alternatives are to maintain existing equipment or replace existing equipment with new equipment. Again, the relevant costs are those which differ among alternatives, and include expected operating costs of new equipment, cash received from disposal of the old equipment, and acquisition cost of the new equipment. The book value of old equipment and any gain or loss on disposal of old equipment are irrelevant. The book value is a past cost which cannot be changed, and gains and losses are not cash items. Exhibits 24-10 and 24-11 in your text illustrate the replacement of equipment decision.

(9) The sell at split-off or process further decision is discussed in detail in objective 4.

OBJECTIVE 3 - EXPLAIN THE DIFFERENCE BETWEEN CORRECT ANALYSIS AND INCORRECT ANALYSIS OF A PARTICULAR BUSINESS DECISION.

Correctly analyzing a business decision requires you to ignore irrelevant costs. A cost that is the same for all decision alternatives is **NOT** relevant and must be ignored. You should consider only those costs and revenues which change between alternatives.

OBJECTIVE 4 - ALLOCATE JOINT PROCESSING COSTS TO JOINT PRODUCTS.

Joint products are separated into identifiable individual products at the split-off point. To be called a joint product, the item must have a significant sales value in relation to the other item produced. For example

Costs incurred before split-off are joint processing costs. They are allocated using the relative sales value method.

$$\text{ALLOCATED COST OF A PRODUCT} = \text{JOINT PROCESSING COST} \times \left[\frac{\text{SALES VALUE OF PRODUCT}}{\text{TOTAL SALES VALUE OF ALL JOINT PRODUCTS}}\right]$$

Study Exhibit 24-13 in your text.

Frequently, a company must decide whether to sell products at the split-off point, or whether to process them further. Joint costs incurred up to this point are not relevant. What is relevant to this decision is the cost of additional processing, called a separable cost, and the extra revenue that is obtained. Exhibit 24-14 in your text illustrates the relevant costs and revenues for this decision.

OBJECTIVE 5 - USE OPPORTUNITY COST IN DECISION MAKING.

An opportunity cost is the profit of the next-best alternative that is given up by selecting a particular alternative. Suppose Alternative A will generate $5,000 income and Alternative B will generate $6,000 income. The opportunity cost of Alternative B is the $5,000 of income from Alternative A that you have given up. Another example of an opportunity cost is the money you might earn from working which you give up to attend the university full-time. An opportunity cost is not associated with a transaction and is therefore not recorded although it must be considered in decision making.

Outlay costs require cash disbursements at some point, and are recorded in the accounting records.

OBJECTIVE 6 - IDENTIFY THREE FACTORS THAT INFLUENCE PRICING DECISIONS.

Three factors that affect pricing decisions are (1) customers, (2) competitors, and (3) costs. Customers must be willing to pay prices that are charged. If competitors sell at lower prices, customers will likely make their purchases from competitors. In the long-run, a company must recover its costs of doing business in order to stay in business.

OBJECTIVE 7 - USE FOUR COST-BASED FORMULAS TO ACHIEVE A DESIRED SALES PRICE.

Prices for products are often marked up from any one of four cost figures. Exhibit 24-15 illustrates several costs. Exhibit 24-16 illustrates four frequently used formulas for calculating markups. These formulas are based on (1) variable manufacturing cost, (2) total variable cost, (3) full total cost, or (4) full absorption cost. Sometimes a percentage is added to the cost number to arrive at the selling price. In other situations, a market selling price is predetermined, and the markup is calculated based on the predetermined selling price and the cost figures.

TEST YOURSELF

All the self-testing materials in this chapter focus on information and procedures that your instructor is likely to test in quizzes and examinations.

I. MATCHING - MATCH EACH NUMBERED TERM WITH ITS LETTERED DEFINITION.

____ 1. Discriminatory pricing

____ 2. full total cost

____ 3. limiting factor

____ 4. outlay cost

____ 5. relevant information

____ 6. split-off point

____ 7. total variable cost

____ 8. full absorption cost

____ 9. joint products

____10. opportunity cost

____11. predatory pricing

____12. separable costs

____13. sunk cost

A. a scheme to temporarily reduce prices in order to eliminate competition and thereby restrict supply, so that prices then may be raised above their original levels

B. a cost that requires a cash distribution sooner or later

C. an actual outlay that has been incurred in the past and is present under all alternatives in a decision

D. charging different prices to different customers for identical services or product

E. costs beyond the split-off point that can be exclusively identified with individual products

F. expected future data that differ between the alternative courses of action in a decision

G. goods that are specifically identified as individual products only after the split-off point

H. the additional cost incurred when one unit of product is manufactured, sold, distributed, and serviced

I. the item that restricts production or sales of a product

J. the maximum available profit contribution foregone by using limited resources for a particular purpose

K. the total of all manufacturing and nonmanufacturing costs; also called fully allocated cost

L. the sum of variable and fixed manufacturing costs

M. the juncture in the production process where goods become specifically identified as individual products

II. MULTIPLE CHOICE - CIRCLE THE CORRECT ANSWER.

1. Relevant information:

   A. is expected future data
   B. differs among alternative courses of action
   C. does not include sunk costs
   D. all of the above

2. The functional format income statement categorizes expenses:

   A. into cost of goods sold and selling and administrative expenses
   B. into variable expenses and fixed expenses
   C. both A and B
   D. neither A nor B

3. The contribution margin format income statement categorizes expenses:

   A. into cost of goods sold and selling and administrative expenses
   B. into variable expenses and fixed expenses
   C. both A and B
   D. neither A nor B

4. Joint cost allocation is most useful for:

   A. the decision to sell now or process further
   B. evaluating the performance of managers
   C. product costing
   D. both A and C

5. The split-off point is the juncture in the production process where:

   A. joint costs are allocated to joint products
   B. separable costs are allocated to joint products
   C. goods become specifically identifiable as individual products
   D. both A and B

III. COMPLETION - COMPLETE EACH OF THE FOLLOWING STATEMENTS.

1. A(n) ______________________________ income statement is more useful for special decision analysis than the standard income statement.

2. The item that restricts production or sales is called the

   ____________________________ or ____________________________________.

3. Fixed costs are only relevant to a special decision if

   ____.

4. A(n) ______________________________ is the cost of the forsaken next best alternative.

5. __________________________________ costs are not formally recorded in the accounting records.

IV. EXERCISES

1. A mail order company has offered to pay $7.00 per unit for 1,000 Easter baskets. This will put idle manufacturing capacity to use and will not affect regular sales. Total fixed costs will not change. There will be only half the normal variable selling and administrative costs on this special order.

Normal selling price per basket	$10.00
Variable costs per basket:	
Manufacturing	5.00
Selling and Administrative	2.00
Fixed costs per basket:	
Manufacturing	.80
Selling and Administrative	1.25

A. What is the relevant information associated with this special order?

B. What difference would accepting this special order have on company profits?

2. Sally, a bright young CPA, has provided you with the following information:

Salary at current position	$ 50,000
Revenues expected by opening her own office	100,000
Expenses expected for the new office	60,000

A. What is the opportunity cost associated with working at her current position?

B. What is the opportunity cost associated with starting her own business?

C. From purely a quantitative standpoint, what should she do?

3. Cicero's Cereals is concerned that operating income is low, and is considering dropping its rice cereal division. The following information is available:

	Total	Wheat Division	Rice Division
Sales	$750,000	$450,000	$300,000
Variable expenses	375,000	183,000	222,000
Contribution margin	$345,000	$267,000	$ 78,000
Fixed expenses	270,000	162,000	108,000
Operating income (loss)	$ 75,000	$105,000	$(30,000)

Cicero can avoid $84,000 of fixed expenses by dropping the Rice Division.

Determine whether Cicero should drop the Rice Division.

SOLUTIONS

I. MATCHING

1. D	2. K	3. I	4. B	5. F	6. M	7. H	8. L	9. G	10. J
11. A	12. E	13. C							

II. MULTIPLE CHOICE

1. D Relevant information is the expected future data that differ between alternative courses of action. A sunk cost is an actual outlay that has been incurred in the past and is present under all alternatives. Sunk costs are irrelevant.

2. A Answer B describes the "contribution margin format" income statement.

3. B Answer A describes the "functional format" income statement.

4. A Answers B and C are incorrect because at the split-off point, joint costs are sunk costs and therefore irrelevant. Thus answer D is also incorrect.

5. C Answer C is the definition of the split-off point. The point at which joint costs are allocated (A) is a management decision. Separable costs (B) are not allocated to joint products.

III. COMPLETION

1. contribution margin
2. limiting factor, constraint
3. fixed costs differ among alternatives
4. opportunity cost
5. Opportunity

IV. EXERCISES

1. A. The relevant information is the special order price of $7.00 per unit, the variable manufacturing cost of $5.00 per unit, and <u>one-half</u> the normal variable selling and administrative expenses which amount to $1.00 per unit ($2 x 1/2).

   B.

Additional revenues from special order (1,000 x $7)	$7,000
Less: Variable manufacturing cost (1,000 x $5)	(5,000)
Less: Variable selling and admin. cost (1,000 x $1)	(1,000)
Increase in profits	$1,000

2. A. The opportunity cost is the net revenue given up by keeping the existing position: $100,000 revenue - $60,000 expense = $40,000.

   B. The opportunity cost is the cost of giving up the existing position: $50,000.

   C. The current position pays $50,000. Going into business will net $40,000. Keeping the present position makes Sally $10,000 better off.

3. The relevant information is the contribution margin that would be lost if the Rice Division is eliminated and the fixed costs that would be eliminated if the Rice Division is closed. The company would lose the $78,000 contribution margin of the Rice Division if it is closed, but would reduce fixed costs by $84,000. The fixed cost savings are $6,000 greater than the lost contribution margin ($84,000 cost saved - $78,000 contribution margin lost), and the division should be closed.

DEMONSTRATION PROBLEM 1: Product to Emphasize; Make or Buy

A. Alpha Co. produces two products, A and B, with the following per unit data:

	Product A	Product B
Selling price	$40	$28
Variable expenses	24	16
Units that can be produced each hour	3	5

The company has 12,000 hours of capacity available. Which product should the company emphasize?

B. John Bush Brush Co. has the following manufacturing costs for 10,000 of its natural bristle brushes:

Direct material	$ 30,000
Direct labor	30,000
Variable overhead	20,000
Fixed overhead	20,000
Total	$100,000

Another manufacturer has offered to sell Bush similar brushes for $8.50 each. By purchasing the brushes outside, Bush can save $9,000 of fixed overhead cost. The released facilities can be devoted to the manufacture of other products that will contribute $6,000 to profits. What is Bush's best decision?

DEMONSTRATION PROBLEM 2: Computing unit costs and target pricing

Susie Sunshine manufactures and sells stuffed toys:

Total budgeted stuffed toys to be produced	550,000
Total fixed nonmanufacturing cost	$2,750,000
Total fixed manufacturing cost	1,650,000
Unit variable nonmanufacturing cost	1
Unit variable manufacturing cost	2

REQUIRED:

1. Compute the following unit costs: Total variable cost, full absorption cost, and full total cost.

2. Compute the markup percentage for each of the three unit costs in Requirement 1 that will yield a desired selling price of $15.

3. Use the percentages you computed in Requirement 2 to compute the $15 selling price by marking up (a) total variable cost and (b) full absorption cost.

25

Capital Budgeting

CHAPTER REVIEW

OBJECTIVE 1 - USE FOUR CAPITAL BUDGETING MODELS TO MAKE INVESTMENT DECISIONS.

Capital budgeting is a long-range investment plan for purchasing, using, and disposing of capital assets such as land, buildings, and machinery.

(1) Payback is the length of time it takes to recover the dollars invested in a capital outlay. If annual cash inflows are identical each year, then:

$$\text{PAYBACK PERIOD} = \frac{\text{AMOUNT INVESTED}}{\text{EXPECTED ANNUAL NET CASH INFLOWS}}$$

If annual cash inflows are not equal, you might construct a table, as in Exhibit 25-2, to determine the payback period. Payback highlights cash inflows, but ignores profitability.

(2) The accounting rate of return measures the average rate of return from using an asset over its entire life:

$$\text{ACCOUNTING RATE OF RETURN} = \frac{\text{AVERAGE ANNUAL OPERATING INCOME FROM INVESTMENT}}{\text{AVERAGE AMOUNT INVESTED}}$$

$$\text{AVERAGE ANNUAL OPERATING INCOME FROM INVESTMENT} = \text{AVERAGE ANNUAL NET CASH INFLOW FROM OPERATIONS} - \text{ANNUAL DEPRECIATION}$$

$$\text{AVERAGE AMOUNT INVESTED} = \frac{\text{AMOUNT INVESTED + RESIDUAL VALUE}}{2}$$

Although the accounting rate of return measures profitability, it ignores the time value of money.

(3) Net present value is a method used to compute expected net monetary gains or losses from a project by discounting expected cash flows to the present value using a desired rate of return. The desired rate of return used to calculate present value is the discount rate or hurdle rate. Exhibit 25-4 in your text illustrates present value analysis in which (1) the annual cash inflows are equal (an annuity) and (2) the annual cash inflows are different. Note that when the annual cash inflows are equal, you use Table 25-2, Present Value of an Annuity of $1, to find the present value factor. When the cash inflows are not equal, you use Table 25-1, Present Value of $1, to find the present value factor for each year of the analysis. Exhibit 25-5 in your text includes in the analysis the residual value of an asset that is expected to be recovered at the end of the asset's useful life.

The steps to determine the net present value of a project are:

(1) Find the present value of annual cash inflows.

(2) Find the present value of the residual, if any.

(3) Add (1) and (2) to obtain the present value of the net cash inflows.

(4) Subtract the investment from the present value of the net cash inflows (3) to obtain the net present value of the project.

The net present value method is based on cash flows and considers both profitability and the time value of money.

The internal rate of return (IRR) of an investment project is the rate of return that makes the net present value of the project equal to zero. The IRR is the rate a company can expect to earn by investing in the project.

The steps to determine the IRR, assuming that annual cash inflows are equal, are:

(1) Identify the expected annual net cash inflows.

(2) Find the interest rate needed to make the present value of cash inflows equal to the present value of cash outflows. Use the following equation to find the appropriate present value of an annuity factor:

Investment = Expected annual net cash inflow X Annuity PV factor

Scan the appropriate row in Table 25-2 which corresponds to the life of the project, and choose the column with the factor closest to the factor you calculated in the equation above. The interest rate in that column is the IRR.

(3) Compare the IRR to the desired rate of return to decide whether or not to accept the project.

If annual cash flows are different, you will have to calculate the present value of cash inflows on a year-by-year basis using Table 25-1 and approximate the IRR.

OBJECTIVE 2 - COMPARE AND CONTRAST POPULAR CAPITAL-BUDGETING MODELS.

Refer to exhibit 25-7 in your text for a list of the strengths and weaknesses of the various capital-budgeting decision models.

OBJECTIVE 3 - DEMONSTRATE HOW INCOME TAXES AFFECT THE CASH FLOWS OF INVESTMENTS.

Taxes are paid on income, yet capital-budgeting techniques focus on cash flow. Differences between income and cash flow arise because of noncash items such as depreciation and gains and losses. Depreciation and losses are not paid in cash, but they reduce taxable income, and therefore decrease cash paid out for income taxes. Gains are not received in cash, but they increase taxable income and therefore increase cash paid out for income taxes.

Refer to the examples in your text and Exhibit 25-8 for illustrations of the various effects depreciation, gains, and losses have on income, taxes, and cash flows.

OBJECTIVE 4 - EXPLAIN THE ROLE OF DEPRECIATION AND BOOK VALUES IN CAPITAL-BUDGETING DECISIONS.

The steps involved in a capital-budgeting decision are to (1) gather information, (2) make cash flow predictions, and (3) use the predictions in a decision model. Refer to Exhibit 25-9 in your text. Book values and depreciation taken in the past do not affect the capital-budgeting decision model. Relevant items include cash outflows for investment projects, tax savings associated with depreciation and losses, and tax expenditures associated with gains.

OBJECTIVE 5 - SHOW HOW ACCELERATED DEPRECIATION AND INVESTMENT TAX CREDITS INCREASE THE NET PRESENT VALUES OF INVESTMENTS.

Accelerated depreciation means we take a larger percentage of depreciation in early years and a smaller percentage in later years. This results in greater tax savings in early years and smaller tax savings in later years. At any interest rate, the present value of cash is greater if the cash is received in early years rather than later years. So accelerated depreciation helps to increase the present value of a project by increasing cash flow in early years.

An investment tax credit reduces taxes when an investment is made. Since most investments are made at the beginning of a project, an investment tax credit reduces taxes immediately, providing an increase in cash flow. Again, this acts to increase the present value of a project.

OBJECTIVE 6 - IDENTIFY THE SPECIAL FEATURES OF INVESTMENTS IN CURRENT ASSETS AND HIGH TECHNOLOGY.

When you spend money to acquire current assets such as inventory you are making an investment. Present value analysis is used for acquiring current assets in the same way as it is used for investments in plant and equipment. The difference is that instead of evaluating the viability of a capital project, you are assessing the cost of holding inventory.

Hi-tech investments present a special problem, since hi-tech projects usually require significant and large investments. Because technology changes so rapidly, a company which does not invest in maintaining state of the art products and production facilities may soon be driven out of business.

OBJECTIVE 7 - DEMONSTRATE THE USE OF SENSITIVITY ANALYSIS IN CAPITAL-BUDGETING DECISIONS.

Sensitivity analysis is used to measure the effect of changing one of the amounts or assumptions from the original present value analysis. It provides the answers to a variety of "what-if" questions that may be asked about an investment analysis.

TEST YOURSELF

All the self-testing materials in this chapter focus on information and procedures that your instructor is likely to test in quizzes and examinations.

I. MATCHING - MATCH EACH NUMBERED TERM WITH ITS LETTERED DEFINITION.

____ 1. accounting rate of return

____ 2. capital budgeting

____ 3. decision model

____ 4. time value of money

____ 5. internal rate of return

____ 6. sensitivity analysis

____ 7. annuity

____ 8. investment tax credit

____ 9. minimum desired rate of return

____10. net present value

____11. payback

____12. MACRS

A. a method or technique for evaluating and choosing among alternative courses of action

B. a special U.S. tax depreciation method that specifies a table of allowable lives and a pattern of allowable depreciation that is geared to the recovery period

C. a "what-if" technique that asks how a result will be changed if an original predicted amount is not achieved or if an underlying assumption changes

D. formal means of making long-range decisions for investments such as plant locations, equipment purchases, additions of product lines, and territorial expansions

E. a direct reduction of income taxes in conjunction with the acquisition of a depreciable asset

F. the average annual income from operations minus the average amount invested to earn the income

G. length of time it will take to recover, in net cash inflows from operations, the dollars of a capital outlay

H. the rate that can be earned by the best alternative use of investment capital

I. the rate of return that makes the net present value of a project equal to zero

J. method of computing the expected net monetary gain or loss from a project by discounting all expected cash flows to their present value, using a minimum desired rate of return

K. stream of equal periodic amounts

L. the fact that one can earn income by investing money for a period of time

II. MULTIPLE CHOICE - CIRCLE THE CORRECT ANSWER.

Use the following information to answer questions 1 - 3:

Cost of machine	$75,000	
Yearly operating income	12,500	
Yearly cash flow	20,000	
Yearly depreciation	7,500	
Life of machine	10	years
Minimum rate of return	8	percent

1. What is the payback period?

   A. 6 years B. 5 years
   C. 10 years D. 3.75 years

2. What is the accounting rate of return?

   A. 33.3 percent B. 26.7 percent
   C. 16.7 percent D. 10 percent

3. What is the net present value of investing in the machine?

   A. $ 8,875
   B. $59,200
   C. $ 2,200
   D. cannot be determined

4. Select the correct statement concerning the payback period.

   A. The longer the payback period, the less attractive the asset.
   B. The shorter the payback period, the less attractive the asset.
   C. The longer the payback period, the more attractive the asset.
   D. Both B and C are correct.

5. The accounting rate of return considers:

   A. the timing of cash flows C. profitability
   B. the time value of money D. all of these

6. The net present value approach to capital budgeting considers:

   A. only cash flows
   B. only the time value of money
   C. both cash flows and the time value of money
   D. the length of time to recoup the initial investment

7. If a potential investment has a negative net present value:

   A. it should be accepted in all situations
   B. it should be rejected in all situations
   C. it should be accepted if payback is less than five years
   D. it should be rejected if the accounting rate of return is less than 16%

III. COMPLETION - COMPLETE EACH OF THE FOLLOWING STATEMENTS.

1. A series of equal periodic payments is called a(n) ____________________.

2. Depreciation, gains, and losses may affect a present value analysis because of the effects of ____________________.

3. In addition to plant and equipment, investments in ____________________ and ____________________ can also use capital-budgeting techniques.

4. ____________________ and ____________________ can increase the net present value of investments.

5. A project's internal rate of return is that rate at which the net present value of the project is ________________________.

6. The major weakness of the payback is that it ____________________________ ____.

7. An investment should be rejected if its net present value is ____.

IV. EXERCISES

1. Donaldson Corp. plans to invest $450,000 in restaurant equipment. Donaldson believes that the investment will generate $40,000 in the first year, $110,000 in the second year, and $120,000 per year thereafter. What is the payback period for this investment? Compute a fraction of a year if necessary.

2. Imbriani Manufacturing is examining a possible investment in some new plastic molding equipment. The Huff. Corp. machine costs $640,000, is expected to generate annual operating income of $85,000, should last for 8 years, and has no residual value. The Heller Equipment Corp. machine costs $900,000 and should last for 10 years. It should generate annual operating income of $105,000, and has an expected residual value of $100,000. Which machine offers the higher accounting rate of return? What is the opportunity cost of purchasing the Heller Equipment Corp. machine?

3. Thayer Company is considering an investment in a mining property. The property has a cost of $226,000. It is expected to yield after-tax cash flow of $40,000 per year for the next 10 years, and has no residual value. Thayer requires an 8 percent return on investments of this type.

   A. What is the net present value of this project?

   B. What is the internal rate of return for this project?

SOLUTIONS

I. MATCHING

1\. F   2. D   3. A   4. L   5. I   6. C   7. K   8. E   9. H   10. J
11\. G   12. B

II. MULTIPLE CHOICE

1\. D $75,000 cost divided by $20,000 annual cash flow is 3.75 years.

2\. A $\frac{12,500}{(75,000 + 0)/2} = .333 = 33.3$ percent

3\. B From table 25-2, the present value of an annuity factor for 8 percent for 10 years is 6.71. Present value of $20,000 X 6.71 is $134,200. $134,200 less the $75,000 cost results in net present value of $59,200.

4\. A Generally, a business wants to recover its investment as quickly as possible. A short payback period is desirable. A longer payback period is undesirable.

5\. C The accounting rate of return is calculated as:

Average Annual Operating Income/Average Amount Invested

The numerator of the equation indicates profitability is the correct answer.

6\. C The net present value method computes the present value of expected future net cash flows and compares that amount to the initial investment. Answer C describes this approach.

7\. B The initial investment is subtracted from the present value of the investment's expected future cash flows. If the result is negative, the investment does not meet the minimum return required. If the result is positive, the investment generates a return above the minimum required. Only projects with positive net present values should be considered.

III. COMPLETION

1. annuity
2. income taxes
3. inventory, high technology
4. accelerated depreciation, investment tax credits
5. equal to zero
6. ignores profitability and the time value of money
7. negative

IV. EXERCISES

1. You must compute payback on a year by year basis:

Cost	$450,000
Cash flow - year 1	(40,000)
Cash flow - year 2	(110,000)
Cash flow - year 3	(120,000)
Cash flow - year 4	(120,000)
Balance after 4 years	60,000

Partial year computation:

Balance remaining/Annual Cash Flow

60,000/120,000

.5 years

Total 4 + .5 = 4.5 years

2.

$$\text{AVERAGE AMOUNT INVESTED} = \frac{\text{AMOUNT INVESTED + RESIDUAL VALUE}}{2}$$

$$\text{ACCOUNTING RATE OF RETURN} = \frac{\text{AVERAGE ANNUAL OPERATING INCOME FROM INVESTMENT}}{\text{AVERAGE AMOUNT INVESTED}}$$

Machine 1: $\text{Average amount invested} = \frac{\$640,000 + \$0}{2} = \$320,000$

$\text{Accounting Rate of Return} = \frac{\$85,000}{\$320,000} = 26.56\ \%$

Machine 2: $\text{Average amount invested} = \frac{\$900,000 + \$100,000}{2} = \$500,000$

$\text{Accounting Rate of Return} = \frac{\$105,000}{\$500,000} = 21\ \%$

3. A.

	PV Factor		Net Cash Inflow	Present Value of Net Cash Inflow
Present value of annual net cash inflows	6.710	X	$40,000	= $260,400
Investment				(226,000)
Net present value of the project				$ 42,400

B.

$$\text{PV factor} = \frac{\text{Investment}}{\text{Expected annual net cash inflows}} = \frac{\$226,000}{\$40,000} = 5.65$$

From Table 25-2 in the row for 10 periods, 5.65 is the PV factor for 12 %.

DEMONSTRATION PROBLEM 1: Capital Budgeting Models

The data for a machine follows:

Cost	$56,400
Estimated annual net cash flows	14,100
Residual value	10,000
Estimated useful life	6 years
Annual rate of return required	10%

The present value of an amount of $1 at 10% in year 6 is 0.564.

The present value of an annuity of $1 at 10% for 6 years is 4.355.

REQUIRED:

1. What is the payback period for the machine?

2. What is the accounting rate of return for the machine?

3. What is the net present value of the machine?

4. Indicate whether each decision model leads to purchase or rejection of this investment. Would you decide to buy the machine? Give your reason.

DEMONSTRATION PROBLEM 2: Tax effects of depreciation on capital budgeting

TransCircuits, Inc. is considering an investment in machinery to manufacture computer memory chips. The machine will cost $1,300,000, and will have a $100,000 disposal value at the end of its three-year life. The machine is expected to generate $600,000 in annual pretax cash operating savings. TransCircuits has an 8 percent cost of capital and a tax rate of 40 percent. Accelerated depreciation amounts permitted by tax law are assumed to be $700,000 in year 1, $400,000 in year 2, and $200,000 in year 3.

The present value of $1 factors at 8 percent are 0.926 for year 1, 0.857 for year 2, and 0.794 for year 3.

The present value of an annuity of $1 at 8 percent for 3 years is 2.577.

REQUIRED:

1. Compute the net present value of the investment using accelerated depreciation.

2. What is the net present value of the investment using straight-line depreciation, assuming that the $100,000 disposal value must be considered when computing depreciation? What is the difference between the net present value using accelerated depreciation and straight-line depreciation, and does this cause the decision to change?

26

Decentralization: Transfer Pricing And Performance Measurement

CHAPTER REVIEW

Management control systems provide a set of rules and techniques to aid and coordinate decision making within a company. Management control systems may promote either centralization or decentralization within a company. The objective of management control is to achieve the objectives of the organization.

OBJECTIVE 1 - IDENTIFY THE BENEFITS AND COSTS OF DECENTRALIZATION.

Decentralization gives managers at lower levels of a company the freedom to make decisions. Decentralization is a matter of degree. An organization's management system may fall anywhere within the range of maximum decentralization to maximum centralization.

The benefits of decentralization include (1) better decisions, (2) faster decisions, (3) greater creativity and motivation, and (4) increased development and learning.

The costs of decentralization include (1) suboptimal decisions, (2) duplication of activities, and (3) higher costs of information.

Suboptimal decisions occur when conflicts arise between the divisional manager's objectives and overall corporate objectives. Goal congruence refers to a situation where harmony exists between divisional goals and overall corporate goals.

OBJECTIVE 2 - CALCULATE THE INCOME OF A COMPANY'S DIVISIONS USING DIFFERENT TRANSFER PRICES.

A transfer price is the price one subunit of an organization charges for a product or service supplied to some other subunit of the same organization. The transfer is revenue to the selling subunit and cost to the buying subunit.

Transfer prices may be based on (1) market prices or (2) the cost of production. Transfer prices based on cost of production may be based on either variable cost or full cost of production. Several different factors affect the determination of transfer prices within the organization.

OBJECTIVE 3 - DETERMINE THE EFFECT OF IDLE CAPACITY ON TRANSFER DECISIONS.

Idle capacity is the ability to produce more units than are needed to satisfy demand for a product. If idle capacity exists, the only additional costs incurred to produce more units are variable costs. With idle capacity, variable cost may be a better guide to setting transfer prices than market price.

If idle capacity does not exist, then market price is often the appropriate transfer price.

When conflicts occur between divisions, some companies allow division mangers to negotiate a mutually acceptable transfer price.

OBJECTIVE 4 - MINIMIZE WORLDWIDE TAXES AND TARIFFS THROUGH TRANSFER-PRICING STRATEGY.

Multinational companies face special tax and tariff considerations. Companies will often ship goods to subsidiaries in high tariff countries at low transfer prices in order to reduce their tariff expenses. Further, companies will often ship goods to subsidiaries in high income tax countries at high transfer prices so as to reduce reported income and taxes in high tax countries.

Complex rules govern tariffs, selling prices, and income taxes. Although restrictions exist, it is difficult for any one country to monitor the worldwide activities of major multinational companies.

OBJECTIVE 5 - COMPUTE THE RETURN ON INVESTMENT, INVESTMENT TURNOVER, AND PROFIT MARGIN OF A DIVISION.

Organizations use a variety of financial and nonfinancial performance measures to evaluate responsibility centers and managers.

Two primary financial performance measures are <u>return on investment (ROI)</u> and <u>residual income</u>.

$$\text{ROI} = \frac{\text{Income}}{\text{Invested Capital}}$$

Return on investment can be divided into two major components - <u>investment turnover</u> and <u>profit margin</u>. Investment turnover is equal to revenue divided by invested capital. Profit margin is equal to income divided by revenue.

ROI = Investment turnover X Profit margin

$$\frac{\text{Income}}{\text{Invested capital}} = \frac{\text{Revenue}}{\text{Invested capital}} \times \frac{\text{Income}}{\text{Revenue}}$$

ROI will increase if investment turnover or the profit margin increases without decreasing the other. Notice from the equation that changes in revenue affect both investment turnover and profit margin, and appear to "cancel out." However, changes in revenue usually result in changes in income, so changes in revenue are not likely to "cancel out" changes; a change in revenue will usually result in a change in income.

Residual income is the income that remains after subtracting the interest you would have to pay if you borrowed the invested capital. This interest amount is called imputed interest.

Residual income = Income - Imputed interest on invested capital

OBJECTIVE 6 - DETERMINE HOW PERFORMANCE MEASURES AFFECT INVESTMENT DECISIONS.

A company may choose to emphasize either ROI or residual income. Residual income tends to emphasize absolute income in dollar terms, while ROI emphasizes income in percentage terms. Residual income supports investment in projects that exceed the cost of capital, while ROI emphasizes those projects that only meet or exceed current ROI.

For example, suppose that the cost of capital is 12 percent, current ROI is 18 percent, and a project exists that will earn 14 percent. Investing at 14 percent will operate to reduce the current 18 percent ROI. Yet the project does exceed the 12 percent cost of capital. A company that emphasizes ROI will not accept the 14 percent project, while a company that emphasizes residual income is more likely to accept the investment.

OBJECTIVE 7 - DISTINGUISH BETWEEN PERFORMANCE OF A DIVISION AND PERFORMANCE OF A DIVISION MANAGER.

The performance of a division may be affected by items beyond the division manager's control. These items are committed fixed costs such as depreciation, property taxes, and insurance over which the division manger has no control. Therefore, many companies evaluate the division manager's performance based on those items which can be controlled by the manager. Refer to Exhibit 26-11 in your text for an example.

The concept of invested capital may also differ from company to company. Assets such as land purchased for future expansion may be assigned to the division, but may not be employed by the division until some future time. Such assets may be excluded when evaluating the performance of the manager, but included when evaluating the division.

TEST YOURSELF

All the self-testing materials in this chapter focus on information and procedures that your instructor is likely to test in quizzes and examinations.

I. MATCHING - MATCH EACH NUMBERED TERM WITH ITS LETTERED DEFINITION.

____ 1. decentralization

____ 2. transfer price

____ 3. goal congruence

____ 4. suboptimal decisions

____ 5. idle capacity

____ 6. return on investment

____ 7. intermediate product

____ 8. residual income

____ 9. investment turnover

____10. profit margin

____11. management control system

____12. multinational company

A. harmony between a subunit manager's goals for the subunit and top management's goals for the overall organization

B. a company that has divisions in more than one country

C. income divided by invested capital

D. the price one subunit of an organization charges for a product or service supplied to another subunit of the same organization

E. income minus imputed interest on invested capital

F. the freedom to make decisions

G. a set of rules and techniques that aid and coordinate decision making within an organization

H. the number of revenue dollars that are generated by each dollar of invested capital

I. production capacity in excess of what is needed to satisfy external customer demand for a division's product

J. the amount of each revenue dollar that goes to income

K. a product transferred from one subunit of a company to another subunit for further processing

L. decisions whose costs to the organization as a whole outweigh the benefits

II. MULTIPLE CHOICE - Circle the correct answer.

1. Income divided by investment capital is

A. profit margin
B. residual income
C. investment turnover
D. return on investment

2. A division of a multinational company is located in a country with a low tariff rate. That division transfers finished goods to a second division located in a country with a high tariff rate. If other factors are equal, the company will minimize its tariff payments if the transfer price is

   A. low
   B. high
   C. determined at arm's-length
   D. based on cost

3. Residual income is

   A. determined by return on investment
   B. income minus imputed interest on invested capital
   C. more popular than return on investment
   D. imputed interest on invested capital minus income

4. When a competitive market exists for a product and there is no idle capacity, optimal decisions usually occur if transfer prices are based on

   A. market price
   B. variable cost
   C. full total cost
   D. fixed cost

5. Which of the following is not a cost of decentralization?

   A. suboptimal decisions
   B. faster decisions
   C. duplication of activities
   D. high costs of information

6. Return on investment is a function of

   A. investment turnover
   B. profit margin
   C. neither A nor B
   D. both A and B

III. COMPLETION - COMPLETE EACH OF THE FOLLOWING STATEMENTS.

1. A multinational company has divisions in ______________________________.

2. When idle capacity exists, transfer prices are usually based on

   ______________________________ or ______________________________________.

3. Return on investment is defined as ___________________________________ times

   ____.

4. ______________________________ describes harmony between subunit goals and overall corporate goals.

5. ___________________________________ is the freedom to make decisions.

6. Decisions whose costs to the organization outweigh the benefits are

   ________________________________ or ________________________________.

7. Companies often resolve transfer pricing conflicts by allowing

   ____.

IV. EXERCISES

1. AMI, Inc. manufactures small electrical appliances. The Parts Division manufactures electrical sockets for lamps and other lighting equipment, while the Lamp Division manufactures a variety of styles of electric lamps. An external market exists for the sockets. The Parts Division currently produces 200,000 sockets per year. The market price for sockets is $6, variable costs are $2 per socket, and fixed costs at the current production level are $1 per socket. The Lamp Division produces 40,000 lamps per year. The market price is $40 per lamp, variable costs not including the socket are $15 per lamp, and fixed costs at the current production level are $9 per lamp.

   A. What is the operating income of each division if the Lamp Division buys sockets from the Parts Division at market price?

   B. What is the operating income of each division if the Lamp Division buys sockets from the Parts Division at 150% of variable cost?

   C. What is the most likely transfer price if no idle capacity exists?

   D. What is the range of acceptable transfer prices if sufficient idle capacity exists to produce all the sockets required by the Lamp Division and the division managers are allowed to negotiate the transfer price?

2. Acme Medical Products Division had revenue of $7,500,000, income of $1,125,000, and invested capital of $6,750,000 last year. Its cost of capital was 8 percent.

   A. Compute investment turnover.

   B. Compute the profit margin.

   C. Compute return on investment.

   D. Compute residual income.

SOLUTIONS

I. MATCHING

1. F 2. D 3. A 4. L 5. I 6. C 7. K 8. E 9. H 10. J
11. G 12. B

II. MULTIPLE CHOICE

1. D The definition of return on investment is income divided by investment capital

2. A Tariffs are usually based on the value of goods. Since the goods are being shipped to a country with high tariffs, the tariff is minimized at a low transfer price

3. B Residual income is defined as income minus imputed interest on invested capital

4. A Market-based prices usually lead to optimal decisions in competitive markets when there is no idle capacity

5. B Faster decisions are a benefit of decentralization, not a cost

6. D Return on investment is investment turnover times profit margin

III. COMPLETION

1. more than one country
2. variable cost, full cost
3. investment turnover, profit margin
4. goal congruence
5. decentralization
6. suboptimal, dysfunctional
7. division managers to negotiate transfer prices

IV. EXERCISES

1. A.

		Parts Division		Lamp Division
Sales	200,000 x $6	$1,200,000	40,000 x $40	$1,600,000
VC	200,000 x 2	(400,000)	40,000 x 15	(600,000)
VC - sockets			40,000 x 6	(240,000)
FC	200,000 x 1	(200,000)	40,000 x 9	(360,000)
Operating income		$ 600,000		$ 400,000

B.

		Parts Division		Lamp Division
Sales	160,000 x $6	$ 960,000	40,000 x $40	$1,600,000
Sales	40,000 x $3[1]	120,000		
VC	200,000 x 2	(400,000)	40,000 x 15	(600,000)
VC - sockets			40,000 x 3[1]	(120,000)
FC	200,000 x 1	(200,000)	40,000 x 9	(360,000)
Operating income		$ 480,000		$ 520,000

[1] Variable cost of $2 x 150 % = $3

C. Market price. The Parts Division will be unwilling to sell any of its output below market price, since it is currently selling all it can produce at the market price.

D. The Lamp Division will not willingly pay more than the market price of $6 per socket. The Parts Division will not willingly sell sockets for less than the variable cost of $2. The price range, then, is a minimum of $2 and a maximum of $6.

2. A. $7,500,000 ÷ $6,750,000 = 1.11

B. $1,125,000 ÷ $7,500,000 = .15 = 15 %

C. 1.11 x 15 % = 16.7 %

D. $1,125,000 - ($6,750,000 x .08) = $585,000

DEMONSTRATION PROBLEM 1

Hokkaido Corp. manufactures CD players, and also the principal component for CD players. The two profit centers are the Component Division and the Consumer Division. The main assembly of the Component Division can be sold to external customers for $60 or transferred to the Consumer Division. The Consumer Division uses the assembly to make a CD player that sells for $250. The variable production costs of the Component Division are $45, while the variable production costs of the Consumer Division are $120.

REQUIRED:

1. If the Component Division has no idle capacity, should transfers be made to the Consumer Division at variable cost? Why or why not?

2. If the Component Division has no idle capacity, will the market price lead to the optimal decision? Explain.

3. Suppose that the Component Division has sufficient idle capacity to produce 2,000 CD assemblies. Will the market price lead to the optimal decision? Explain.

4. If idle capacity exists, and the two division managers are allowed to negotiate a transfer price, in what range will it fall? What is the minimum price the Component Division will accept, and what is the maximum price the Consumer Division will pay?

5. Suppose that the Component Division is located in Hong Kong and the Consumer Division is located in the United States. The income tax rate in Hong Kong is 20 percent, while the U.S. tax rate is 35 percent. How much more or less tax per unit will Hokkaido pay if the transfer price is $90 instead of $60?

<u>Requirement 1</u>

Requirement 2

Requirement 3

Requirement 4

Requirement 5

DEMONSTRATION PROBLEM 2: Performance Measurement

The Beverage Division of Home Foods Co. sold 200,000 cases of carbonated beverages last year for $6 per case. Its variable costs were $4 per case, and fixed costs amounted to $250,000. The capital invested in the division was $750,000, and its cost of capital was 12 percent.

REQUIRED:

1. Compute the Beverage Division's investment turnover, profit margin, and ROI.

2. Compute the division's residual income.

3. Management is considering adding a line of mineral water, with an expected ROI of 15%. Will management be inclined to add the line if it is evaluated based on ROI? On residual income? Explain.

4. Two proposals exist for improving ROI. One is to raise the selling price to $6.50 per case. The other is to reduce invested capital to $700,000. Calculate the effect on turnover, profit margin, and ROI for each of these proposals independently, assuming no other changes.

5. Which proposal is more effective in increasing ROI? Why?

<u>Requirement 1</u>

<u>Requirement 2</u>

Requirement 3

Requirement 4

Requirement 5

Using Accounting Information To Make Business Decisions

CHAPTER REVIEW

OBJECTIVE 1 - PERFORM A HORIZONTAL ANALYSIS OF COMPARATIVE FINANCIAL STATEMENTS.

Financial statement analysis is based on information taken from the annual report, SEC reports, articles in the business press, and so on. The objective of financial statement analysis is to provide information to creditors and investors to help them (1) predict future returns and (2) assess the risk of those returns. Past performance is often a good indicator of future performance. Three categories of financial statement analysis are: horizontal, vertical, and ratio analysis.

The study of percentage changes in comparative statements is called **horizontal analysis.** Horizontal analysis highlights changes over time. Computing a percentage change in comparative statements requires two steps: (1) compute the dollar amount of the change from the base period to the later period, and (2) divide the dollar amount of the change by the base period amount.

The base period for horizontal analysis is the year prior to the year being considered. Suppose there are three years of data. The change from Year 1 to Year 2 is:

$$\frac{\$\ \text{YEAR 2} - \$\ \text{YEAR 1}}{\$\ \text{YEAR 1}}$$

and the change from Year 2 to Year 3 is:

$$\frac{\$\ \text{YEAR 3} - \$\ \text{YEAR 2}}{\$\ \text{YEAR 2}}$$

No percentage changes are computed if the base-year amount is zero or negative.

Trend percentages are a form of horizontal analysis. They indicate the direction of business activities by comparing numbers over a span of several years. Trend percentages are computed by selecting a base year and expressing the amount of each item for each of the following years as a percentage of the base year's amount for that item.

OBJECTIVE 2 - PERFORM A VERTICAL ANALYSIS OF FINANCIAL STATEMENTS.

Vertical analysis of a financial statement reveals the percentage of the total that each statement item represents. Percentages on the comparative income statement are computed by dividing all amounts by net sales. Percentages on the comparative balance sheet are shown as either (1) a percentage of total assets or (2) a percentage of total liabilities and stockholders' equity.

Vertical analysis of the income statement highlights changes in such items as the gross profit percentage and net income.

Vertical analysis of the balance sheet shows the composition of balance sheet items. Trend analysis can be used to highlight year-to-year percentage changes.

OBJECTIVE 3 - PREPARE COMMON-SIZE FINANCIAL STATEMENTS.

Common-size statements report amounts in percentages only. The common-size statement is a form of vertical analysis. On a common-size income statement, each item is expressed as a percentage of the net sales amount. In the balance sheet, the common-size is the total on each side of the accounting equation. Note that common-size percentages are the same percentages shown on financial statements using vertical analysis.

Common-size percentages can be used to compare financial statements of different companies, or to compare one company's financial statements to industry averages.

OBJECTIVE 4 - USE THE STATEMENT OF CASH FLOWS IN DECISION MAKING.

The statement of cash flows presents the cash effects of operating, investing, and financing activities.

Questions to consider might include:

(1) Does the company generate the majority of its cash from operations, from selling fixed assets or from borrowing?

(2) Does the company retain enough income to finance future operations?

OBJECTIVE 5 - COMPUTE THE STANDARD FINANCIAL RATIOS USED FOR DECISION MAKING.

A ratio is the mathematical relationship of one number to another number.

Working capital is used to measure a business's ability to meet its short-term obligations with its current assets.

$$\text{WORKING CAPITAL} = \text{CURRENT ASSETS} - \text{CURRENT LIABILITIES}$$

The current ratio is used to measure the availability of sufficient liquid assets to maintain normal business operations.

$$\text{CURRENT RATIO} = \frac{\text{CURRENT ASSETS}}{\text{CURRENT LIABILITIES}}$$

The acid-test (quick) ratio measures the ability of a business to pay all of its current liabilities if they came due immediately.

$$\text{ACID-TEST RATIO} = \frac{\text{CASH} + \text{SHORT-TERM INVESTMENTS} + \text{NET CURRENT RECEIVABLES}}{\text{CURRENT LIABILITIES}}$$

Remember that inventory and prepaid expenses are not used to compute the acid-test ratio.

Inventory turnover is a measure of the number of times a company sells its average level of inventory during a year.

$$\text{INVENTORY TURNOVER} = \frac{\text{COST OF GOODS SOLD}}{\text{AVERAGE INVENTORY}}$$

$$\text{AVERAGE INVENTORY} = \frac{\text{BEGINNING INVENTORY} + \text{ENDING INVENTORY}}{2}$$

Accounts receivable turnover measures the ability of a company to collect cash from its credit customers.

$$\text{ACCOUNTS RECEIVABLE TURNOVER} = \frac{\text{NET CREDIT SALES}}{\text{AVERAGE NET ACCOUNTS RECEIVABLE}}$$

$$\text{AVERAGE NET ACCOUNTS RECEIVABLE} = \frac{\text{BEGINNING ACCOUNTS RECEIVABLE} + \text{ENDING ACCOUNTS RECEIVABLE}}{2}$$

Days' sales in receivables measures in sales days the value of accounts receivable; it tells how many days' sales remain uncollected (in accounts receivable).

$$\text{ONE DAY'S SALES} = \frac{\text{NET SALES}}{\text{365 DAYS}}$$

$$\text{DAYS' SALES IN AVERAGE ACCOUNTS RECEIVABLE} = \frac{\text{AVERAGE NET ACCOUNTS RECEIVABLE}}{\text{ONE DAY'S SALES}}$$

To compute the ratio for the beginning of the year, substitute beginning net Accounts Receivable for average net Accounts Receivable. To compute the ratio for the end of the year, substitute ending net Accounts Receivable for average net Accounts Receivable.

The debt ratio measures the relationship between total liabilities and total assets.

$$\text{DEBT RATIO} = \frac{\text{TOTAL LIABILITIES}}{\text{TOTAL ASSETS}}$$

The times-interest-earned ratio measures the ability of a business to pay interest expense.

$$\text{TIMES-INTEREST-EARNED RATIO} = \frac{\text{INCOME FROM OPERATIONS}}{\text{INTEREST EXPENSE}}$$

Remember that income from operations **does not include** interest revenue, interest expense, or income tax expense.

Return on sales measures the relationship between income and sales.

$$\text{RATE OF RETURN ON NET SALES} = \frac{\text{NET INCOME}}{\text{NET SALES}}$$

Return on assets measures the success a company has in using its assets to earn a profit.

$$\text{RATE OF RETURN ON ASSETS} = \frac{\text{NET INCOME + INTEREST EXPENSE}}{\text{AVERAGE TOTAL ASSETS}}$$

$$\text{AVERAGE TOTAL ASSETS} = \frac{\text{BEGINNING TOTAL ASSETS + ENDING TOTAL ASSETS}}{2}$$

The <u>rate of return on common stockholders' equity</u> shows the relationship between net income and common stockholders' investment in the company.

$$\text{RATE OF RETURN ON COMMON STOCKHOLDERS' EQUITY} = \frac{\text{NET INCOME - PREFERRED DIVIDENDS}}{\text{AVERAGE COMMON STOCKHOLDERS' EQUITY}}$$

$$\text{AVERAGE COMMON STOCKHOLDERS' EQUITY} = \frac{\text{BEGINNING + ENDING COMMON STOCKHOLDERS' EQUITY}}{2}$$

<u>Earnings per share (EPS)</u> is the amount of net income per share of the company's common stock.

$$\text{EPS} = \frac{\text{NET INCOME - PREFERRED DIVIDENDS}}{\text{NUMBER OF SHARES OF COMMON STOCK OUTSTANDING}}$$

The <u>price/earnings ratio</u> is the ratio of the market price of a share of common stock to the company's EPS.

$$\text{PRICE/EARNINGS RATIO} = \frac{\text{MARKET PRICE PER SHARE OF COMMON STOCK}}{\text{EARNINGS PER SHARE}}$$

<u>Dividend yield</u> is the ratio of dividends per share of stock to the stock's market price per share.

$$\text{DIVIDEND YIELD ON COMMON STOCK} = \frac{\text{DIVIDEND PER SHARE OF COMMON STOCK}}{\text{MARKET PRICE PER SHARE OF COMMON STOCK}}$$

The formula for calculating <u>book value per share of common stock</u> is:

$$\text{BOOK VALUE PER SHARE OF COMMON STOCK} = \frac{\text{TOTAL STOCKHOLDERS' EQUITY - PREFERRED EQUITY}}{\text{NUMBER OF SHARES OF COMMON STOCK OUTSTANDING}}$$

OBJECTIVE 6 - USE RATIOS IN DECISION MAKING.

Ratios should be (1) evaluated over a period of years, and (2) compared to industry standards.

When a problem is found, the items used to compute the ratio should be analyzed to determine the nature of the problem. At that time, possible solutions to the problem can be suggested.

In an <u>efficient capital market</u>, stock prices reflect all information that is available to the public.

TEST YOURSELF

All the self-testing materials in this chapter focus on information and procedures that your instructor is likely to test in quizzes and examinations.

I. MATCHING - MATCH EACH NUMBERED TERM WITH ITS LETTERED DEFINITION.

____ 1. accounts receivable turnover

____ 2. working capital

____ 3. common size statements

____ 4. days' sales in receivables

____ 5. dividend yield

____ 6. inventory turnover

____ 7. return on total assets

____ 8. times-interest-earned ratio

____ 9. vertical analysis

____10. acid-test ratio

____11. current ratio

____12. debt ratio

____13. horizontal analysis

____14. price/earnings ratio

____15. return on net sales

____16. book value per share of common stock

____17. return on common stockholders' equity

A. analysis of a financial statement that reveals the relationship of each statement item to the total which is the 100 percent figure

B. common stockholders' equity divided by the number of shares of common stock outstanding

C. current assets divided by current liabilities

D. current assets minus current liabilities

E. financial statements that report only percentages (no dollar amounts)

F. measures the number of times that operating income can cover interest expense

G. measures the number of times a company sells its average level of inventory during a year

H. ratio of the market price of a share of common stock to the company's earnings per share

I. measures the success a company has in using its assets to earn a profit

J. net income minus preferred dividends, divided by average common stockholders' equity; a measure of profitability

K. ratio of average net accounts receivable to one day's sales

L. ratio of dividends per share to the stock's market price per share

M. ratio of net income to net sales; a measure of profitability

N. study of percentage changes in comparative financial statements

O. tells the proportion of a company's assets that it has financed with debt

P. tells whether an entity could pay all its current liabilities if they came due immediately

Q. the ratio of net credit sales to average net accounts receivable; it measures ability to collect cash from credit customers

II. MULTIPLE CHOICE - CIRCLE THE CORRECT ANSWER.

1. In vertical analysis the relationship between cost of goods sold and net sales is shown by the:

   A. income from operations percentage
   B. net income percentage
   C. gross profit percentage
   D. net sales percentage

2. Which of the following measures profitability?

   A. debt ratio
   B. current ratio
   C. dividend yield
   D. earnings per share of common stock

3. Which of the following current assets is <u>not</u> used to compute the acid-test ratio?

   A. Accounts Receivable
   B. Cash
   C. Inventory
   D. Short-term Investments

4. Which of the following is a common measure of a firm's ability to meet short-term obligations?

   A. working capital
   B. rate of return on sales
   C. net assets
   D. price/earnings ratio

5. The times-interest-earned ratio measures:

   A. profitability
   B. ability to pay interest expense on debt
   C. ability to pay current liabilities
   D. ability to collect receivables

6. The proportion of a firm's assets financed by debt is measured by the:

   A. current ratio
   B. debt ratio
   C. debt yield ratio
   D. times-interest-earned ratio

7. Assume that a company's current ratio is greater than one. If the company pays current liabilities with cash, the new current ratio will:

   A. increase
   B. decrease
   C. remain unchanged
   D. cannot be determined

III. COMPLETION - COMPLETE EACH OF THE FOLLOWING STATEMENTS.

1. The study of percentage changes in comparative financial statements is called ______________________________ analysis.

2. Vertical analysis percentages on the income statement are computed by dividing all amounts by ______________________________.

3. Vertical analysis percentages on the balance sheet are computed by dividing all amounts by ______________________________.

4. Working capital is ______________________________ ______________________________.

5. ______________ and ______________ are the two most common measures of firm size.

6. Leverage ______________________________ the risk to common stockholders.

7. The ______________ ratio indicates the market price of one dollar of earnings.

8. The rate of return on total assets equals ______________________________ ______________________________.

9. The most widely quoted of all financial statistics is ______________________________ ______________________________.

10. The ______________________________ is the recorded accounting value of each share of common stock outstanding.

IV. EXERCISES

1. Net income was $100,000 in Year 1 and $150,000 in Year 2. What was the percentage increase in net income?

2. Ratio Inc. had the following information for 19X1:

Cost of Goods Sold	$350,000
Beginning Inventory	40,000
Ending Inventory	120,000
Net Credit Sales	500,000
Beginning Accounts Receivable	50,000
Ending Accounts Receivable	70,000

A. What is the inventory turnover?

B. What is the accounts receivable turnover?

C. What is the days' sales in average receivables?

3. The following information is given for Hannah Co. for 19X9:

Net Sales	$ 675,000
Net Income	450,000
Average Common Stockholders' Equity	2,400,000
Average Total Assets	2,925,000
Interest Expense	45,000
Preferred Dividends	30,000
Common Dividends	15,000
Common Stock Outstanding	240,000 shares

A. What is the rate of return on net sales?

B. What is the rate of return on total assets?

C. What is the rate of return on common stockholders' equity?

4. The following information is given for Jack Frost Corporation:

Assets:	
Cash	$ 80,000
Marketable Securities	144,000
Accounts Receivable	168,000
Inventory	72,000
Equipment	360,000
Total	$824,000
Liabilities and Stockholders' Equity	
Accounts Payable	$ 84,000
Salary Payable	32,000
Long-Term Bonds Payable	120,000
Common Stock	150,000
Retained Earnings	438,000
Total	$824,000

A. What is the current ratio?

B. What is the acid-test (quick) ratio?

C. What is the debt ratio?

5. Murkey Water Co. has a price/earning ratio of 22, dividends of $3.60 per share, and earnings per share of $1.65.

A. What is the market price per share?

B. What is the dividend yield?

SOLUTIONS

I. MATCHING

1. Q	2. D	3. E	4. K	5. L	6. G	7. I	8. F	9. A	10. P
11. C	12. O	13. N	14. H	15. M	16. B	17. J			

II. MULTIPLE CHOICE

1. C The gross profit percentage is:

   (Net Sales - Cost of Goods Sold) / Net Sales

2. D Debt ratio measures ability to pay long-term debts. Current ratio measures ability to pay current liabilities. Dividend yield is used in analyzing stock as an investment.

3. C Only the most liquid current assets are used to calculate the acid-test ratio. Inventory must be sold and resultant receivable collected, thus it is not considered to be very liquid.

4. A Working capital is current assets less current liabilities. It measures a firm's ability to meet short term obligations.

5. B Times-interest-earned measures how many times greater is operating income than interest expense.

6. B Current ratio measures ability to pay current liabilities. Debt yield ratio has no meaning. Times-interest-earned ratio measures ability to pay interest on debt. The debt ratio is: total liabilities ÷ total assets.

7. A Let CA = current assets, CL = current liabilities, and X = the amount of cash paid on current liabilities. Then given that $CA > CL$ (or $CL < CA$), show that:

$$\frac{(CA - X)}{(CL - X)} > \frac{CA}{CL}$$

$$CL(CA - X) > CA(CL - X)$$

$$CL*CA - CL*X > CA*CL - CA*X$$

$$- CL*X > CA*X$$

   divide by - X: $CL < CA$

   NOTE: In a firm with current assets greater than current liabilities, the current ratio can be improved by using cash to pay current liabilities.

III. COMPLETION

1. horizontal
2. net sales
3. total assets (or total liabilities plus owners' equity)
4. current assets minus current liabilities
5. net sales, total assets
6. increases
   (Leverage is the practice of increasing the debt financing of an entity with respect to owner financing. Leverage is a two edged sword, increasing profits (and returns to shareholders') during good times but compounding losses during bad times.)
7. price/earnings
8. (net income plus interest expense) / average total assets
9. earnings per share
10. book value per share of common stock

IV. EXERCISES

1. ($150,000 / $100,000) / $100,000

2. A. $$\frac{\text{COST OF GOODS SOLD}}{\text{AVERAGE INVENTORY}} = \frac{\$350,000}{(\$40,000 + \$120,000) / 2} = 4.375$$

   B. $$\frac{\text{NET CREDIT SALES}}{\text{AVERAGE ACCOUNTS RECEIVABLE}} = \frac{\$500,000}{(\$50,000 + \$70,000) / 2} = 8.333$$

   C. $$\frac{\text{AVERAGE ACCOUNTS RECEIVABLE}}{\text{ONE DAY'S SALES}} = \frac{(\$50,000 + \$70,000) / 2}{\$500,000 / 365} = 43.8 \text{ Days}$$

3. A. $$\frac{\text{NET INCOME}}{\text{NET SALES}} = \frac{\$450,000}{\$675,000} = .667$$

   B. $$\frac{\text{NET INCOME + INTEREST EXPENSE}}{\text{AVERAGE TOTAL ASSETS}} = \frac{\$45,000}{\$2,925,000} = .169$$

   C. $$\frac{\text{NET INCOME - PREFERRED DIVIDENDS}}{\text{AVERAGE COMMON STOCKHOLDERS' EQUITY}} = \frac{\$450,000 - \$30,000}{\$2,400,000} =.175$$

4. A. $$\frac{\text{CURRENT ASSETS}}{\text{CURRENT LIABILITIES}} = \frac{\$80,000 + \$144,000 + \$168,000 + \$72,000}{\$84,000 + \$32,000} = 4$$

   B. $$\frac{\text{CASH + SHORT-TERM INVESTMENTS + NET CURRENT RECEIVABLES}}{\text{CURRENT LIABILITIES}} =$$

   $$\frac{\$80,000 + \$144,000 + \$168,000}{\$84,000 + \$32,000} = 3.379$$

   C. $$\frac{\text{TOTAL LIABILITIES}}{\text{TOTAL ASSETS}} = \frac{\$84,000 + \$32,000 + \$120,000}{\$824,000} = .286$$

5. A. $$\frac{\text{MARKET PRICE PER SHARE OF COMMON STOCK}}{\text{EARNINGS PER SHARE}} = \frac{P}{\$1.65} = 22$$

   P = $36.30

   B. $$\frac{\text{DIVIDENDS PER SHARE OF COMMON STOCK}}{\text{MARKET PRICE PER SHARE OF COMMON STOCK}} = \frac{\$3.60}{\$36.30} = .099$$

DEMONSTRATION PROBLEM

Chaykin Corporation common stock is currently trading on the open market at $8 per share. The company balance sheets and earnings statements for 19X1 and 19X2 are provided below:

Chaykin Corporation
Balance Sheets
Years 19X2 and 19X1

	19X2	19X1
Assets		
Current assets:		
Cash	$ 13,300	$ 20,350
Marketable securities, at cost (same as short-term investments)	8,200	8,000
Receivables, net	26,000	24,000
Inventories	45,000	40,000
Prepaid expenses	2,500	4,650
Total current assets	95,000	97,000
Property, plant, and equipment, net	185,680	196,500
Land	40,000	35,000
Intangibles and other assets	2,400	2,400
	$323,080	$330,900
Liabilities and Stockholders' Equity		
Current liabilities:		
Notes payable	$ 10,000	$ 10,500
Current installments of long-term debt	3,550	3,445
Accounts payable-trade	14,447	18,500
Accrued liabilities	3,670	1,605
Total current liabilities	31,667	34,050
Long-term debt, less current installments	95,500	93,330
Capital lease obligations, less current portion	1,100	2,150
Deferred income and deferred income taxes	4,813	4,370
Total common stockholders' equity (shares outstanding: 110,000 at year-end 19X2 and 100,000 at year-end 19X1)	190,000	197,000
	$323,080	$330,900

Chaykin Corporation
Statements of Earnings
Years 19X2 and 19X1

	19X2	19X1
Total revenue	$416,500	$406,316
Costs and expenses:		
Costs of products sold	322,593	315,812
Selling, administrative, and general expenses	41,219	43,200
	363,812	359,012
Earnings from operations	52,688	47,304
Interest expense	3,251	3,150
Earnings before income taxes	49,437	44,154
Income taxes	7,437	6,554
Net earnings	$ 42,000	$ 37,600

REQUIRED:

Compute each of the following ratios for Chaykin Corporation for the year 19X2:

1. Current Ratio
2. Acid-Test Ratio
3. Inventory Turnover
4. Days' Sales in Average Receivables
5. Accounts Receivable Turnover
6. Debt Ratio
7. Times-Interest-Earned Ratio
8. Rate of Return on Sales (Total Revenue)
9. Rate of Return on Total Assets
10. Rate of Return on Common Stockholders' Equity
11. Price/Earnings Ratio
12. Book Value Per Share of Common Stock

1. Current Ratio

2. Acid-Test Ratio

3. Inventory Turnover

4. Days' Sales in Average Receivables

5. Accounts Receivable Turnover

6. Debt Ratio

7. Times-Interest-Earned Ratio

8. Rate of Return on Net Sales

9. Rate of Return on Total Assets

10. Rate of Return on Common Stockholders' Equity

11. Price/Earnings Ratio

12. Book Value Per Share of Common Stock

13. Dividend Yield

Solutions

CHAPTER 16 DEMONSTRATION PROBLEM SOLVED AND EXPLAINED

1. Sales Budget

	July	August	September	Total
Cash sales (10%)	$ 5,000	$ 7,000	$ 3,000	$ 15,000
Credit sales (90%)	45,000	63,000	27,000	135,000
Total sales	$50,000	$70,000	$30,000	$150,000

Sales for each month consist of 10% cash sales and 90% credit sales. Multiply each month's sales by the appropriate percentage to obtain budgeted cash and budgeted credit sales.

2. Purchases, Cost of Goods Sold, and Inventory Budget

	July	August	September	Total
Cost of goods sold[1]	$20,000	$28,000	$12,000	$60,000
+ Desired ending inventory[2]	16,800	7,200	6,000[5]	6,000
Subtotal	$36,800	$35,200	$18,000	$66,000
- Beginning inventory[3]	12,000[4]	16,800	7,200	12,000
= Purchases	$24,800	$18,400	$10,800	$54,000

[1] Budgeted cost of goods sold is 40% of budgeted sales: $2 ÷ $5 = 40%.

[2] Desired ending inventory is 60% of the following month's cost of goods sold.

[3] Beginning inventory is 60% of the current month's cost of goods sold.

[4] The beginning inventory for July is the balance from the June 30 balance sheet.

[5] To find desired ending inventory for September, it is necessary to compute October's cost of goods sold:

October's Cost of Goods Sold = .4 X $25,000 = $10,000
Desired ending inventory = .6 X $10,000 = $6,000

3. Operating Expenses Budget

	July	August	September	Total
Sales commissions	$ 2,500	$ 3,500	$ 1,500	$ 7,500
Depreciation	4,000	4,000	4,700	12,700
Insurance	3,000	3,000	3,000	9,000
Other operating expenses	12,000	22,000	18,000	52,000
Total operating expenses	$21,500	$32,500	$27,200	$81,200

Sales commissions are 5% of the budgeted sales for each month, paid in the month of the sale. Other operating expenses are given in the problem.

4. Budgeted Cash Disbursements for Purchases

	July	August	September
Current month	$17,360	$12,880	$ 7,560
Previous month	6,000*	7,440	5,520
Total disbursements for purchases	$23,360	$20,320	$13,080

Disbursements for purchases are budgeted at 70% in the month of purchase, and 30% in the following month. Multiply the budgeted purchases from the Purchases, Cost of Goods Sold, and Inventory Budget in Part 2 above by the appropriate percentage to obtain budgeted cash disbursements.

* The $6,000 disbursement relating to previous month's purchases is 30% X $20,000 of June purchases.

5. Budgeted Cash Disbursements for Operating Expenses

	July	August	September
Sales commissions	$ 2,500	$ 3,500	$ 1,500
Insurance	3,000	3,000	3,000
Other operating expenses:			
Current month	6,000	11,000	9,000
Previous month	5,000*	6,000	11,000
Total disbursements for operating expenses	$16,500	$23,500	$24,500

Accounts for commissions, insurance, and other operating expenses are taken from the Operating Expense Budget in Part 3. Disbursements for operating expenses are made at the rate of 50% of current month's operating expenses and 50% of previous month's operating expenses.

* Total Accounts Payable balance on June 30 less amount owed for purchases ($11,000 - $6,000).

6. Schedule of Cash Collections

	July	August	September	Total
Cash sales	$ 5,000	$ 7,000	$ 3,000	$ 15,000
Collection of credit sales:				
Current month	27,000	37,800	16,200	81,000
Previous month	10,800*	28,000	25,200	54,000
Total cash collections	$42,800	$62,800	$44,400	$150,000

Cash sales for each month are 10% of the month's budgeted sales. The remaining 90% of sales are credit sales, collected 60% in the month of sale, and 40% the following month.

* Accounts receivable balance on June 30.

7. Cash Budget

	July	August	September
Beginning cash balance	$ 5,000	$ 7,940	$ 4,170
+ Cash collections	42,800	62,800	44,400
= Cash available	$47,800	$70,740	$48,570
Cash disbursements:			
Purchases	$23,360	$20,320	$13,080
Operating expenses	16,500	23,500	24,500
Equipment	0	25,750	0
Total disbursements	$39,860	$69,570	$37,580
Ending cash balance before financing	7,940	1,170	10,990
- Minimum cash desired	4,000	4,000	4,000
Cash excess (deficiency)[1]	$ 3,940	($ 2,830)	$ 6,990
Financing:			
Borrowings (beginning of month)		$ 3,000	
Repayments (end of month):			
Principal			$3,000
Interest	0	0	30
Ending balance[2]	$ 7,940	$ 4,170	$ 7,960

[1] (Ending cash before financing - minimum cash desired)

[2] The ending balance for July is the cash excess plus the minimum cash desired: $3,940 + $4,000 = $7,940; or, it is the ending cash balance before financing.

The ending balance for August is the ending balance before financing plus the borrowing: $1,170 + $3,000 = $4,170.

The ending balance for September is the ending cash balance before financing minus the principal repayment minus the interest payment: $10,990 - $3,000 - $30 = $7,960.

8. McGregor's Seeds
Budgeted Income Statement
For the Quarter Ended September 30, 19X9

Sales[1]		$150,000
Cost of goods sold[2]		60,000
Gross profit		$ 90,000
Operating expenses[3]:		
Sales commissions	$ 7,500	
Depreciation	12,700	
Insurance	9,000	
Other expenses	52,000	81,200
Income from operations		$ 8,800
Interest expenses[4]		30
Net income		$ 8,770

[1] Budgeted sales are obtained from the Sales Budget in Part 1.

[2] Budgeted cost of goods sold is obtained from the Purchases, Cost of Goods Sold, and Inventory Budget in Part 2.

[3] Operating expenses are obtained from the Operating Expense Budget in Part 3.

[4] Interest expense is obtained from the Cash Budget in Part 4.

9.

McGregor's Seeds
Budgeted Balance Sheet
September 30, 19X9

ASSETS		LIABILITIES	
Cash[1]	$ 7,960	Accounts payable[5]	$ 12,240
Accounts receivable[2]	10,800		
Inventory[3]	6,000	OWNER'S EQUITY	
Building and equipment (net)[4]	103,050		
		McGregor, capital[6]	115,570
Total Assets	$127,810	Total liabilities and owner's equity	$127,810

[1] The cash balance is obtained from the Cash Budget in Part 7.

[2] Ending accounts receivable is equal to the unpaid balance of September's credit sales: .4 X $27,000 = $10,800.

[3] Inventory is equal to the ending inventory balance from the Purchases, Cost of Goods Sold, and Inventory Budget in Part 2.

[4] The ending balance for building and equipment is equal to the beginning balance of building and equipment plus the truck purchased minus depreciation: $90,000 + $25,750 - $12,700 = $103,050.

[5] The ending balance of accounts payable is the sum of the 30% balance of budgeted September purchases plus the 50% balance of budgeted September operating expenses: (.3 X $10,800) + $9,000 = $12,240.

[6] The ending balance in McGregor's Capital account is equal to the balance on June 30 plus budgeted net income for the quarter: $106,800 + $8,770 = $115,570.

CHAPTER 17 DEMONSTRATION PROBLEM SOLVED AND EXPLAINED

Requirement 1

To compute break-even sales in dollars and in units, we need to find the contribution margin per unit and the contribution margin ratio:

Contribution Margin Per Unit = Sales Price Per Unit - Variable Expense Per Unit

Contribution Margin Percentage or Ratio = $\frac{\text{Contribution Margin}}{\text{Sales Price per Unit}}$

Since variable expenses are 60% (.6) of sales, the contribution margin per unit is:

$40 - (.6 X $40) = $40 - $24 = $16

The contribution margin ratio is:

$16 ÷ $40 = .4

The computation of break-even sales in units is:

Break-Even Sales in Units = $\frac{\text{Fixed Expenses}}{\text{Contribution Margin Per Unit}}$

$400,000 ÷ $16 = 25,000 robots

The break-even point in units is 25,000 robots.

The computation of break-even sales in dollars is:

Break-Even Sales in Dollars = $\frac{\text{Fixed Expenses}}{\text{Contribution Margin Percentage}}$

$400,000 ÷ .4 = $1,000,000

The break-even point in dollars is $1,000,000.

Requirement 2

The target operating income is given as $80,000. The number of robots that must be sold to earn a target income of $80,000 is:

Target Sales in Units = $\frac{\text{Fixed Expenses + Target Operating Income}}{\text{Contribution Margin Per Unit}}$

($400,000 + $80,000) ÷ $16 = 30,000 robots

To achieve the target operating income of $80,000, 30,000 robots must be sold.

Requirement 3

To find the solution to requirement 4, you must first determine exactly what item changes. No change in fixed expenses is indicated, and the target operating income of $80,000 remains the same. However, the selling price increases from $40 to $48, an increase of $8. Since variable expenses are not mentioned, you must assume that variable expenses remain at $24 per unit. Since *only* the selling price of the robot has changed, we must find the new contribution margin per unit in order to use the formula for target sales in units in requirement 3. The new contribution margin per unit is:

$48 - $24 = $24

Since the contribution margin per unit has increased to $24, the new target sales in units will be:

($400,000 + $80,000) ÷ $24 = 20,000 robots

Target sales in units has decreased to 20,000 units. This is due to the increase in the selling price and the resulting increase in the contribution margin per unit.

Requirement 4

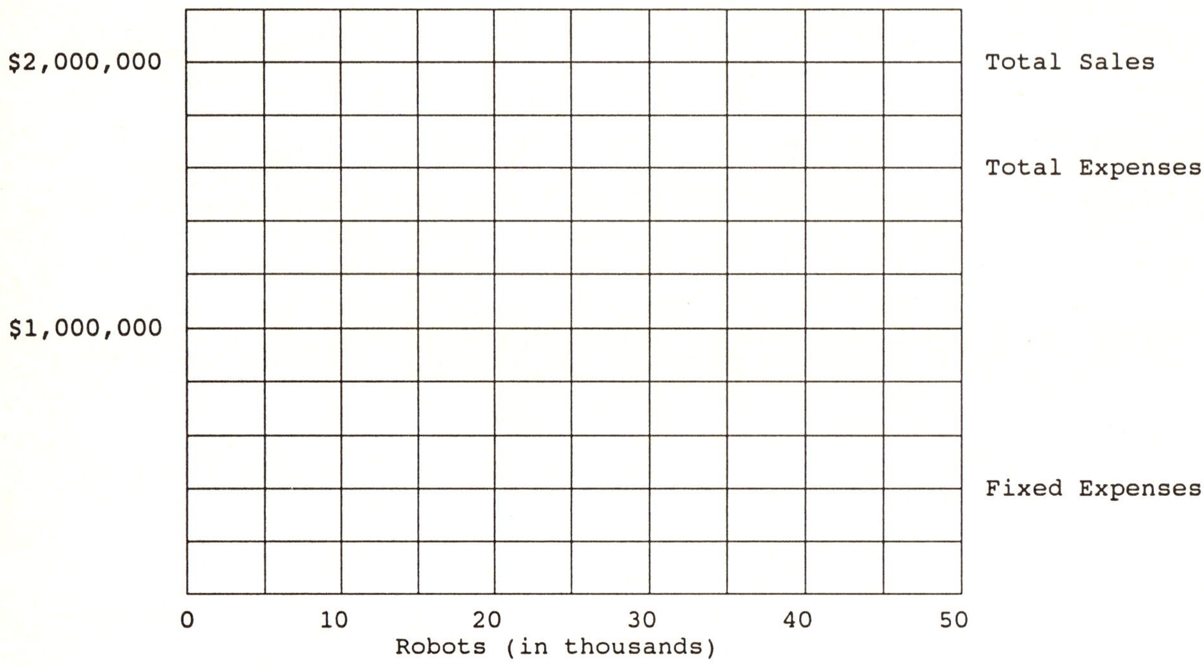

Since the robot sells for $40, at 50,000 units total sales in dollars will be $2,000,000 ($40 X 50,000). In requirement 1, we determined that total fixed expenses were $400,000. Thus, the fixed expense line will be a horizontal line as indicated on the graph. Variable expenses are $24 per unit, so total variable expenses at 50,000 robots will be $1,200,000 ($24 X 50,000). At zero volume, total expenses will be $400,000 ($00,000 fixed expenses plus $0 variable expenses). At volume of 50,000 robots, total expenses will be $1,600,000 ($400,000 fixed and $1,200,000 variable).

As the graph indicates, the break-even point is 25,000 robots or $1,000,000. At 30,000 units, total sales will be $1,200,000, and total expenses will be $1,120,000 ($400,000 fixed and $720,000 variable), leaving targeted operating income of $80,000.

Part B

Outer Space Toys Company
Contribution Margin Income Statement
For the Year 19X9

Sales revenue (35,000 X $40)		$1,400,000
Variable expenses:		
Cost of goods sold ($1,400,000 X .6 X .55)	$462,000	
Operating expenses ($1,400,000 X .6 X .45)	378,000	840,000
Contribution margin		$ 560,000
Fixed expenses:		
Operating expenses (given)		400,000
Income from operations		$ 160,000

The important point to remember when preparing the Contribution Margin Income Statement is that total variable expenses are 60% (.6) of total sales. On the contribution margin income statement, we typically separate variable expenses into cost of goods sold and operating expense components. In this problem, 55% of total variable expenses are attributed to cost of goods sold, and 45% of total variable expenses are attributed to operating expenses.

CHAPTER 18 DEMONSTRATION PROBLEM 1 SOLVED AND EXPLAINED

Part A

<u>Requirement 1</u>

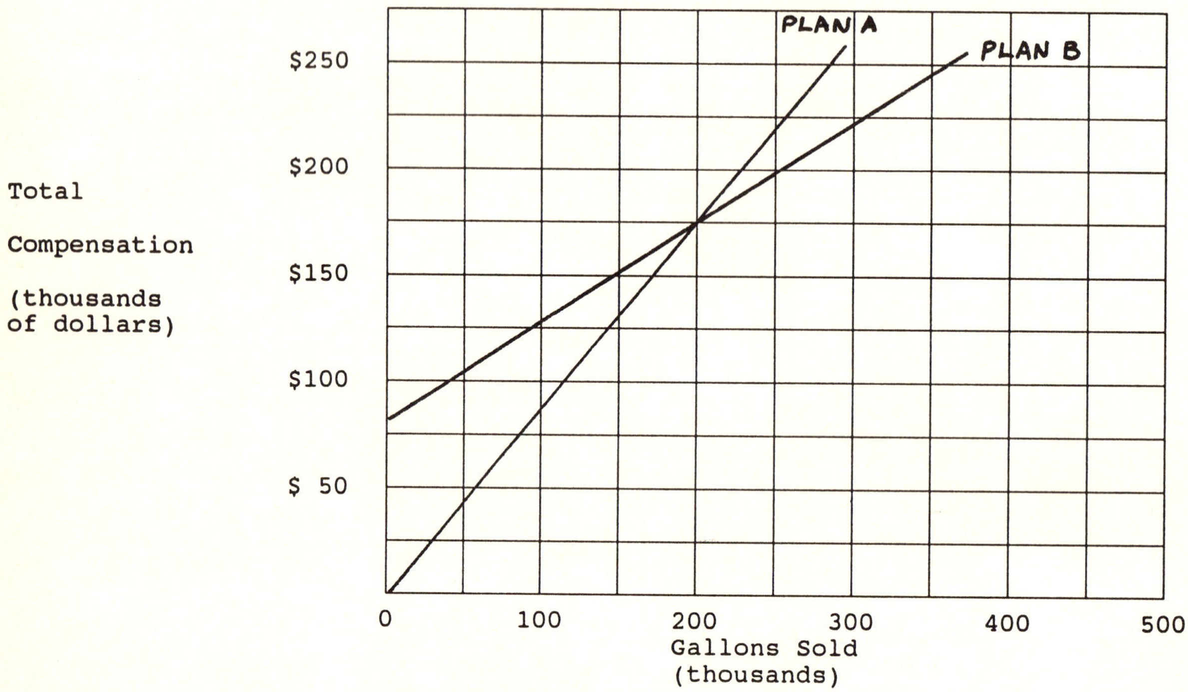

<u>Requirement 2</u>

Plan A total compensation = Plan B total compensation

$.888 X gallons sold = $44,400 X 2 salespersons + $0.444 X gallons sold

($0.888 - $0.444) X gallons sold = $88,800

$0.444 X gallons sold = $88,800

gallons sold = 200,000

Part B

Requirements 1 and 2

	Plan A	Plan B
Sales revenue (1,110,000 gal. X $22.20)	$24,642,000	$24,642,000
Sales commissions		
(1,110,000 X $0.888)	985,680	
(1,110,000 X $0.444)		492,400
Other variable expenses		
(1,110,000 X $13,32)	14,785,200	14,785,200
Contribution margin	$ 8,871,120	$ 9,363,960
Sales salary expense	---	88,800
Other fixed expense	2,664,000	2,664,000
Operating income	$ 6,207,120	$ 6,611,160

CHAPTER 18 DEMONSTRATION PROBLEM 2 SOLVED AND EXPLAINED

Requirements 1 and 2

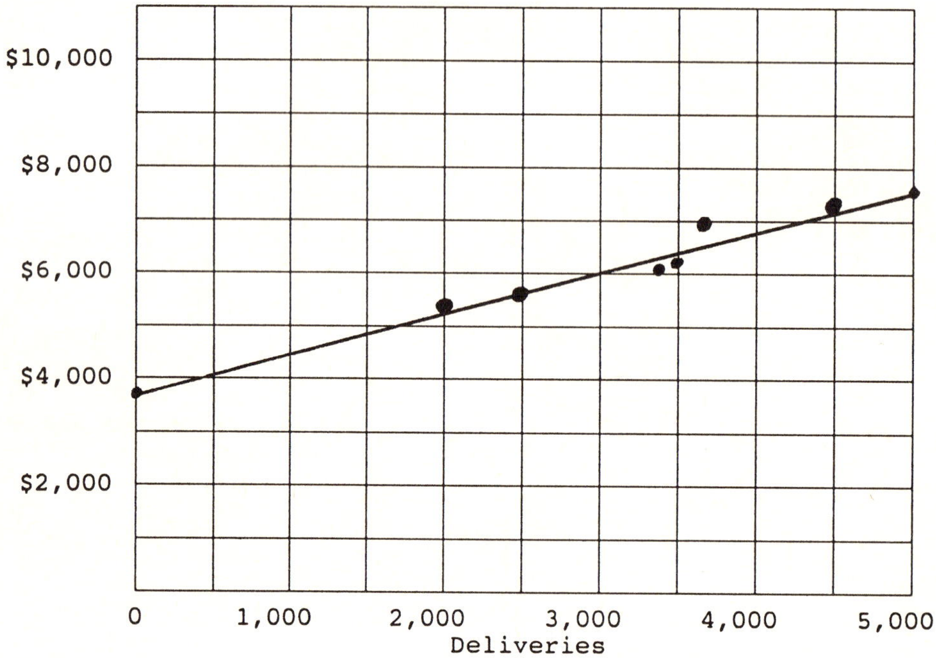

Requirement 3

The high level of activity and costs occurs in the third month; and the low level of activity and costs occur in the fifth month.

$$\text{Variable rate} = \frac{\text{Change in costs}}{\text{Change in volume}} = \frac{\$7,200 - \$5,420}{4,500 - 2,000} = \frac{\$1,780}{2,500}$$

= \$0.712 per delivery

Fixed component = Total mixed cost - Variable component

At the high point: = \$7,200 - (\$0.712 X 4,500)

= \$7,200 - \$3,204

= \$3,996

At the low point: = \$5,420 - (\$0.712 X 2,000)

= \$5,420 - \$1,424

= \$3,996

Because the high point of the sample falls below the regression line and the low point is above it, the high-low cost function has a slope that is less steep ($0.712 versus $0.752) and a higher fixed-cost component ($3,996 versus $3,930). The high-low equation predicts higher costs at low volume levels (below 1,650 deliveries) and lower costs at higher volume levels.

Requirement 4

High-low prediction:

Total cost = $3,996 + ($0.712 X 4,100)

= $3,996 + $2,919

= $6,915

Regression prediction:

Total cost = $3,930 + ($0.752 X 4,100)

= $3,930 + $3,083

= $7,013

CHAPTER 19 DEMONSTRATION PROBLEM SOLVED AND EXPLAINED

<u>Requirement 1</u> (record transactions)

		Debit	Credit
A.	Materials Inventory	37,500	
	Accounts Payable		37,500
B.	Work in Process Inventory	50,000	
	Materials Inventory		50,000
C.	Factory Overhead	2,760	
	Materials Inventory		2,760
D.	Factory Wages	16,000	
	Wages Payable		16,000
	Work in Process Inventory (.75 X $16,000)	12,000	
	Factory Overhead (.25 X $16,000)	4,000	
	Factory Wages		16,000
E.	Factory Overhead	6,015	
	Accumulated Depreciation		700
	Accounts Payable		5,315
F.	Work in Process Inventory (.25 X $50,000)	12,500	
	Factory Overhead		12,500
G.	Finished Goods Inventory	87,725	
	Work in Process Inventory		87,725
H.	Cost of Goods Sold	109,290	
	Finished Goods Inventory		109,290
	Accounts Receivable	153,060	
	Sales Revenue		153,060
I.	Cost of Goods Sold	345	
	Factory Overhead (see T-account)		345

<u>Points to Remember</u>:

In transaction D, it is important to distinguish between direct labor and indirect labor. Direct labor is 75% of the total factory wages of $16,000, or $12,000. The remaining $4,000 is indirect labor.

In transaction F, it is important to note that overhead is applied based on <u>direct materials</u>. The only direct materials in this problem are the $50,000 of direct materials in transaction B.

To prepare the entry for item I, it is necessary to know the balance in the Factory Overhead account:

Factory Overhead

Debit		Credit	
(C)	2,760		
(D)	4,000		
(E)	6,015		
		(F)	12,500
Bal.	345		
		(J)	345
Bal.	0		

Since the account has a debit balance, we credit it in order to bring its balance to zero.

<u>Requirement 2</u> (inventory balances)

Materials

Debit		Credit	
Beg.	60,000		
(A)	37,500		
		(B)	50,000
		(C)	2,760
Bal.	44,740		

Work in Process

Debit		Credit	
Beg.	26,015		
(B)	50,000		
(D)	12,000		
(F)	12,500		
		(G)	87,725
Bal.	12,790		

Finished Goods

Debit		Credit	
Beg.	37,650		
(G)	87,725		
		(H)	109,290
Bal.	16,085		

To find the ending balances, just post the transactions to T-accounts.

<u>Requirement 3</u>

A debit balance in the Factory Overhead account indicates that Factory Overhead is **underapplied.** The T-account in requirement 1 indicates that Factory Overhead had a debit balance of $345 prior to closing the account to Cost of Goods Sold.

<u>Requirement 4</u>

Review the T-account analysis below. Remember that Cost of Goods sold <u>includes</u> the posting from underapplied or overapplied factory overhead.

Cost of Goods Sold

Debit		Credit
(H)	109,290	
(J)	345	
Bal.	109,635	

CHAPTER 20 DEMONSTRATION PROBLEM SOLVED AND EXPLAINED

Requirement 1

Use the 5-step process costing system to solve this problem.

Steps 1 & 2

Flow of Production in Physical Units
and Equivalent Units of Production
Coloring Department
For the Month Ended April 30, 19XX

Flow of Production	Flow of Physical Units	Equivalent Units: Transferred In	Materials	Conversion
Units to account for:				
Work in process, March 31	30,000			
Transferred in	140,000			
Total units to account for	170,000			
Units accounted for:				
Completed and transferred out in April:				
From beginning inventory	30,000		24,000[2]	18,000[3]
Transferred in and completed	90,000[1]	90,000	90,000	90,000
Total transferred out	120,000			
Ending inventory	50,000	50,000	20,000[4]	25,000[5]
Total units accounted for	170,000	140,000	134,000	133,000

[1] A total of 120,000 units were transferred out according to the problem. Since 30,000 of those units were from beginning inventory, the balance of 90,000 were transferred in and completed during the period. Since these are completed units, each completed unit equals one equivalent unit, and the completed units are carried across to the equivalent unit computation.

Total transferred out - Beginning inventory = Transferred in and completed

120,000 - 30,000 = 90,000 units

[2] The Beginning Work in Process Inventory was 20% complete with respect to direct materials. Therefore, 80% of the direct materials were added during April to the physical units in beginning inventory (100% - 20%).

.8 X 30,000 = 24,000 equivalent units

[3] The Beginning Work in Process Inventory was 40% complete with respect to conversion. Therefore, 60% of the conversion was performed on Beginning Work in Process Inventory during April (100% - 40%).

.6 X 30,000 = 18,000 equivalent units

[4] The problem states that 40% of the direct materials had been added during April to the physical units remaining in ending inventory.

.4 X 50,000 = 20,000 equivalent units

[5] The problem states that 50% of the conversion had been performed during April on the physical units remaining in ending inventory.

.5 X 50,000 = 25,000 equivalent units

<u>Steps 3 & 4</u>

Computation of Unit Cost
Coloring Department
For the Month Ended April 30, 19XX

	Transferred-In Costs	Materials	Conversion	Total
Work in process, March 31 (Costs for work done before April)				$ 73,910
Costs added in April	$210,000	$ 18,760	$273,980	502,740
Divide by Equivalent units	÷140,000	÷134,000	÷133,000	
Cost per equivalent unit	$ 1.50	$ .14	$ 2.06	
Total cost to account for:				$576,650

<u>Points to Remember</u>:

When computing unit costs, the costs from the prior period are <u>not included</u> in the computation of unit costs. The unit cost for each cost category is equal to the costs added to that category during the period divided by the equivalent units for that category, which were computed in Step 2.

<u>Step 5</u>

Application of Total Cost to Units Completed
and Units in Ending Work in Process
Coloring Department
For the Month Ended April 30, 19XX

	Transferred-In Costs	Materials	Conversion	Total
Units completed and transferred out to Finished Goods Inventory:				
From work in process, March 31				$ 73,910
Costs added during April:				
Direct materials	-	24,000 X $.14		3,360
Conversion costs	-		18,000 X $2.06	37,080
Total completed from beginning inventory				114,350
Units transferred in and completed during April	90,000 X ($1.50 + $.14 + $2.06)			333,000
Total costs transferred out				$447,350
Work in process, April 30:				
Transferred-in costs	50,000 X $1.50			$ 75,000
Direct materials		20,000 X $.14		2,800
Conversion costs			25,000 X $2.06	51,500
Total work in process, April 30				129,300
Total costs accounted for				$576,650

Points to Remember:

Units Completed and Transferred Out

Units from Work in Process, March 31:

The problem states that $73,910 of cost was associated with the March 31 work in process balance. The FIFO process costing method always assumes that costs associated with beginning work in process are the first costs to be transferred out in the next period.

Costs added during April:

Whenever beginning work in process exists, it is necessary to compute the balance of costs incurred to complete the work. According to the problem, additional materials and conversion were needed to complete the beginning work in process. The equivalent units were computed in Step 2, and the unit costs for each category were determined in Step 3. The amount of cost to complete beginning work in process is the equivalent units times the unit cost. A separate computation is made for (1) direct materials and (2) conversion costs.

Units Transferred-In and Completed during April:

Since transferred-in and completed units are 100% complete, separate computations for each of the cost categories are not necessary. The cost associated with units transferred-in and completed in the same period will equal the number of units times the sum of the unit costs of (1) transferred-in costs, (2) direct materials, and (3) conversion.

Ending Work in Process, April 30:

To compute the balance of ending work in process, it is necessary to make a separate computation for (1) transferred-in costs, (2) direct materials, and (3) conversion. For each of the costs, the balance in ending work in process will equal the equivalent units of production from Step 2 times the unit cost from Step 3.

Once the costs have been applied, you should compare the total costs accounted for in Step 5 with the total cost to account for from Step 4. In both cases the amount in this problem is $576,650.

Requirement 2

Use the 5-step process costing system to solve this problem.

Steps 1 & 2

Flow of Production in Physical Units
and Equivalent Units of Production
Coloring Department
For the Month Ended April 30, 19XX

Flow of Production	Flow of Physical Units	Equivalent Units		
		Transferred In	Materials	Conversion
Units to account for:				
Work in process, March 31	30,000			
Transferred in	140,000			
Total units to account for	170,000			
Units accounted for:				
Completed and transferred out in April:	120,000	120,000	120,000	120,000
Ending inventory	50,000	50,000	20,000[1]	25,000[2]
Total units accounted for	170,000			
Equivalent units		170,000	140,000	145,000

1 The problem states that 40% of the direct materials had been added during April to the physical units remaining in ending inventory.

.4 X 50,000 = 20,000 equivalent units

2 The problem states that 50% of the conversion had been performed during April on the physical units remaining in ending inventory.

.5 X 50,000 = 25,000 equivalent units

Steps 3 & 4

Computation of Unit Cost
Coloring Department
For the Month Ended April 30, 19XX

	Transferred-In Costs	Materials	Conversion	Total
Work in process Mar. 31	$ 48,400	$ 2,240	$ 23,270	$ 73,910
Costs added in April	210,000	18,760	273,980	502,740
Total cost	$258,400	$ 21,000	$297,250	
Divide by Equivalent units	÷170,000	÷140,000	÷145,000	
Cost per equivalent unit	$ 1.52	$ .15	$ 2.05	
Total cost to account for:				$576,650

Points to Remember:

When computing unit costs, the costs from the prior period are included in the computation of unit costs. The unit cost for each cost category is equal to the beginning inventory costs plus added to that category during the period all divided by the equivalent units for that category, which were computed in Step 2.

Step 5

Application of Total Cost to Units Completed
and Units in Ending Work in Process
Coloring Department
For the Month Ended April 30, 19XX

	Transferred-In Costs	Materials	Conversion	Total
Units completed and transferred out to Finished Goods Inventory:				
120,000 X ($1.52 + $0.15 + $2.05)				$446,400
Work in process, April 30:				
Transferred-in costs	50,000 X $1.52			$ 76,000
Direct materials		20,000 X $.15		3,000
Conversion costs			25,000 X $2.05	51,250
Total work in process, April 30				130,250
Total costs accounted for				$576,650

Points to Remember:

Units Completed and Transferred Out

The weighted average method combines costs associated with beginning inventory and costs incurred during the current period.

Equivalent units are computed based on units completed during the period and units remaining in ending work in process inventory. With the weighted average method, it does not matter whether the units were started in the prior period or in the current period.

Thus, the cost of units completed will equal the number of units times the sum of the unit costs of (1) transferred-in costs, (2) direct materials, and (3) conversion.

Ending Work in Process, April 30:

To compute the balance of ending work in process, it is necessary to make a separate computation for (1) transferred-in costs, (2) direct materials, and (3) conversion. For each of the costs, the balance in ending work in process will equal the equivalent units of production from Step 2 times the unit cost from Step 3.

Once the costs have been applied, you should compare the total costs accounted for in Step 5 with the total cost to account for from Step 4. In both cases the amount in this problem is $576,650.

CHAPTER 21 DEMONSTRATION PROBLEM SOLVED AND EXPLAINED

Part A

Requirement 1 - (income statement performance report)

Strawser's Straw Hat Co.
Income Statement Performance Report
For the Year Ended December 31, 19X9

	(1)	(2)	(3)	(4)	(5)
		(1) - (3)		(3) - (5)	
	Actual Results at Actual Prices	Flexible Budget Variances	Flexible Budget for Actual Volume Achieved	Sales Volume Variances	Static (Master) Budget
Units	25,500	-0-	25,500	1,500 F	24,000
Sales	$235,875	$6,375 U	$242,250	$14,250 F	$228,000
Variable expenses	109,825	2,375 F	112,200	6,600 U	105,600
Fixed expenses	57,570	3,570 U	54,000	-	54,000
Total expenses	167,395	1,195 U	166,200	6,600 U	159,600
Operating income	$ 68,480	$7,570 U	$ 76,050	$7,650 F	$ 68,400

Explanations:

Column 1

Column 1 contains actual results that were presented in the body of the problem.

Column 3

Column 3 contains the flexible budget for the volume actually sold. Actual sales were 25,500 hats. Budgeted revenue is $242,250 ($9.50 per hat x 25,500 hats). Budgeted variable expenses are $112,200 ($4.40 x 25,500 hats). Budgeted revenue and budgeted variable expenses may be calculated by multiplying units actually sold by the budget formula amounts in the flexible budget. Note that fixed expenses of $54,000 are constant at all the production levels presented in the flexible budget.

Column 5

The amounts in column 5 are the static, or master budget, amounts. The problem notes that the static budget is based on 24,000 units, a volume level also found in the flexible budget.

Column 2

The flexible budget variances are the differences between actual results (column 1) and flexible budget amounts (column 3). When revenue or income is greater than budgeted, the variance is favorable. When revenue or income is less than budgeted, the variance is unfavorable. For example, the flexible budget variance for sales is $6,375 U (actual sales were less than the flexible budget amount). It may be helpful to think of revenues and income as desirable. Obtaining more of a desirable item is favorable, while obtaining less is unfavorable. When expenses are greater than budgeted, the variance is unfavorable. When expenses are less than budgeted, the variance is favorable. For example, the flexible budget variance for variable expenses is $2,375 F (actual variable expenses were less than the flexible budget amounts). It may help to remember that spending less than planned is favorable, while spending more is unfavorable.

Column 4

Sales volume variances are the differences between flexible budget amounts for actual sales and static budget amounts. Note that no sales volume variance exists for fixed expenses, since fixed expenses are constant at the various levels of sales given in the problem. The criteria to determine whether the variances are favorable or unfavorable is the same as detailed in the explanation for column 2.

Requirement 2 (reconciling variances)

Static (master) budget operating income............	$68,400
Actual operating income at actual prices...........	68,480
Total difference to account for..............	$ 80 F

Note that when actual operating income is greater than static budget operating income, the variance is favorable.

Sales volume variance..............................	$ 7,650 F
Flexible budget variance...........................	7,570 U
Total net variance..........................	$ 80 F

Since the favorable sales volume variance is greater than the unfavorable flexible budget variance, the overall net variance is favorable.

Part B

Requirement 1

Price Variances

A price variance is the difference between actual and budgeted unit prices of inputs times the actual quantity of inputs used. The actual price for direct materials was $.65 per pound and the standard price was $.70 per pound. Materials used amounted to 26,200 pounds.

Direct materials price variance = ($.65 - $.70) x 26,200 = $1,310 F

The direct materials price variance is favorable because the actual price of $.65 is less than the budgeted (standard) price of $.70.

The actual rate paid for direct labor was $7.40 per hour and the standard rate was $7.20 per hour. Total labor amounted to 6,300 hours.

Direct labor price variance = ($7.40 - $7.20) x 6,300 = $1,260 U

The direct labor price variance is unfavorable because the actual price of $7.40 is greater than the standard price of $7.20.

Efficiency Variances

An efficiency variance is the difference between the amount of inputs actually used and the inputs that should have been used for the production times the standard unit price of the input. Actual usage of direct materials was 26,200 pounds and standard usage was 25,500 pounds.

Direct materials efficiency variance = (26,200 - 25,500) x $.70 = $490 U

The direct materials efficiency variance is unfavorable because the actual quantity of 26,200 pounds used was greater than the standard quantity of 25,500 pounds that should have been used to make 25,500 hats.

The actual labor usage was 6,300 hours. The standard input was 1/4 hour, and 25,500 hats were sold. The standard amount of labor for 25,500 hats is 6,375 hours (1/4 x 25,500).

Direct labor efficiency variance = (6,300 - 6,375) x $7.20 = $540 F

The direct labor efficiency variance is favorable because the 6,300 actual hours used were less than the standard 6,375 hours that should have been used.

<u>Requirement 2</u> (overhead variances)

Total overhead variance:

Total actual overhead cost (variable, $23,700 + fixed, $34,900)	$58,600
Standard total overhead applied to production (6,375 hours x $10)	63,750
	$ 5,150 F

The total overhead variance measures the difference between total actual overhead and the standard overhead applied to production. Remember that standard overhead applied to production is a function of the inputs that should have been used for the production that occurred, and not actual inputs associated with production.

Flexible budget variance:

Total actual overhead cost ($23,700 + $34,900)	$58,600
Total flexible budget overhead for actual production (variable, $25,500 + fixed, $36,000)	61,500
	$ 2,900 F

The flexible budget variance measures the difference between total actual overhead cost and the amount of budgeted overhead based on the flexible budget for the level of production which did occur. Remember that the flexible budget changes as production changes, and the change is generally associated with variable expenses.

Production volume variance:

Flexible budget overhead for actual production ($25,500 + $36,000)	$61,500
Standard overhead applied to production (6,375 x $10)	63,750
	$ 2,250 F

The production volume variance measures the difference between flexible budgeted overhead and overhead actually applied to production. Note that the sum of the flexible budget variance ($2,900 F) and the production volume variance ($2,250 F) is equal to the total overhead variance ($5,150 F).

Requirement 3

Strawser's Straw Hat Co.
Income Statement
For the Year Ended December 31, 19X9

Sales revenue				$235,875
Cost of goods sold at standard cost (direct materials $17,850, direct labor $45,900, applied overhead $63,750)			$127,500	
Cost variances:	Favorable	Unfavorable		
Direct materials price	$1,310	$ 0		
Direct materials efficiency		490		
Direct labor price		1,260		
Direct labor efficiency	540			
Overhead flexible budget	2,900			
Overhead production volume	2,250			
	$7,000	$1,750		
Net cost variance			($ 5,250)	
Cost of goods sold at actual cost				122,250
Gross profit				113,625
Selling and administrative				45,145
Operating income				$ 68,480

Points to Remember:

When you prepare an income statement using standard cost of goods sold, do not use actual cost of goods sold. Instead, use the flexible budget amounts for direct materials and direct labor, and the applied amount for overhead. Then schedule the variances as above. In this problem, the total of the favorable variances are greater than the total of the unfavorable variances, and the net cost variance is favorable. A favorable net cost variance reduces cost of goods sold at standard, while an unfavorable net cost variance increases cost of goods sold at standard.

CHAPTER 22 DEMONSTRATION PROBLEM 1 SOLVED AND EXPLAINED

Department	Square Feet Occupied	x	Weight	=	Weighted Value of Space	Proportion of weighted space	Allocation of $60,000 Rent	Rent Expense Per Foot
Men's	4,400	x	1.0	=	4,400	.275	$16,500	$3.75
Women's	4,000	x	2.0	=	8,000	.5	30,000	7.50
Children's	6,000	x	0.6	=	3,600	.225	13,500	2.25
Total	14,400				16,000		$60,000	

Explanation:

In order to allocate the rent, it is necessary to compute the weighted value of the space occupied by each department. Multiply the actual square footage occupied by each department times its assigned weight. The men's department is considered average, so it is assigned a weight of 1.

Once the weighted value of the space has been determined, the next step is to compute the proportion of weighted space for each department. Divide the weighted value of space for each department by the total weighted value. For the men's department, the proportion is .275 (4,400 ÷ 16,000).

The next step is to allocate rent. Multiply the proportion for each department by the total rent of $60,000. For the men's department, the allocation is $16,500 (.275 x $60,000).

The final step is to compute rent expense per square foot. Divide the allocated portion of rent by the actual space occupied for each department. For the women's department, the rent expense per square foot is $7.50 ($30,000 ÷ 4,000).

CHAPTER 22 DEMONSTRATION PROBLEM 2 SOLVED AND EXPLAINED

Home-Office Journal

		Debit	Credit
A.	Branch Ledger Control	4,000	
	Accounts Payable		4,000
B.	no entry		
C.	Branch Ledger Control	7,900	
	Cash		7,900
D.	no entry		
E.	Finished Goods Inventory	14,400	
	Branch Ledger Control		14,400
F.	Accounts Receivable	20,000	
	Sales		20,000
	Cost of Goods Sold	6,000	
	Finished Goods Inventory		6,000
G.	Cash	17,800	
	Accounts Receivable		17,800

Branch Journal

A.	Direct Materials Inventory	4,000	
	Home-Office Ledger Control		4,000
B.	Work in Process Inventory	3,600	
	Direct Materials Inventory		3,600
C.	Factory Wages	7,900	
	Home-Office Ledger Control		7,900
D.	Work in Process Inventory	3,950	
	Factory Overhead Control		3,950
E.	Home-Office Ledger Control	14,400	
	Work in Process Inventory		14,400
F.	no entry		
G.	no entry		

Explanations:

A. The home office is responsible for liabilities, but the branch is responsible for direct materials. Therefore the home office records the liability and the branch records the direct materials inventory. Both the home office and the branch use their respective reciprocal accounts.

B. Only the branch is responsible for production, and only the branch makes an entry. Responsibility for the transaction is not divided between the home office and the branch.

C. The home office is responsible for cash payments, but the branch is responsible for factory wages. The home office records the cash payment and the branch records the factory wages. Both the home office and the branch use their respective reciprocal accounts.

D. This entry is the responsibility of the branch for the reasons explained in explanation B above.

E. The home office controls finished goods, but the branch must remove the cost of finished goods from work in process. Responsibility is divided, and both the home office and the branch make entries.

F. Sales and cost of sales are the responsibility of the home office. Only the home office makes an entry.

G. Collection of accounts receivable is the responsibility of the home office. Only the home office makes an entry.

CHAPTER 23 DEMONSTRATION PROBLEM 1 SOLVED AND EXPLAINED

Requirement 1

Direct materials 500 engines X $5,000	$2,500,000
Conversion costs of activities:	
Purchasing 800 purchase orders X $75	60,000
Assembly 500 engines X 1280 parts X $5	3,200,000
Testing 500 engines X 10 hrs X $25	125,000
Total cost	$5,885,000
Divide by the number of engines	500
Average cost per unit	$ 11,770

Requirement 2

Cost	$5,885,000
Markup 30% X $5,885,000	1,765,500
Bid	$7,760,500

Requirement 3

Direct materials 500 engines X $5,000	$2,500,000
Conversion costs:	
100,000 DLH X $31	3,100,000
Total cost	$5,600,000

Cost	$5,600,000
Markup 30% X $5,600,000	1,680,000
Bid	$7,280,000

CHAPTER 23 DEMONSTRATION PROBLEM 2 SOLVED AND EXPLAINED

Requirement 1

Average sales price	$1,200
Desired manufacturing contribution	450
Allowable costs	$ 750

Requirement 2

Allowable costs	$750
Kaizen cost reduction	50
Target cost	$800

Target cost	$800
Value engineering cost reduction goal	120
Initial budgeted cost	$920

Requirement 3

a. Internal failure
b. Prevention
c. Appraisal
d. External failure

CHAPTER 24 DEMONSTRATION PROBLEM 1 SOLVED AND EXPLAINED

A. Product to Emphasize

		Product A	Product B
(1)	Units that can be produced each hour	3	5
(2)	Contribution margin per unit*	X $16	X $12
(3)	Contribution margin per hour (1) X (2)	$48	$60
	Capacity: Number of hours	X 15,000	X 15,000
	Total contribution margin for capacity	$576,000	$720,000

* Contribution margins: A: $40 - $24 = $16; B: $28 - $16 = $12

Decision: The company should emphasize Product B because its contribution margin at capacity is greater by $144,000.

Explanation:

When a constraint exists, such as the number of labor hours available, we must conduct our profit analysis in terms of the constraint. Since only 12,000 labor hours are available, our profit will be greatest if we produce those products which offer the highest contribution margin per labor hour. To compute the contribution margin per labor hour for each product, multiply the contribution margin per unit of each product times the number of units of each product that can be produced per hour. The product with the highest contribution margin per hour will provide the highest profit.

B. Make or Buy

	Alternatives		
	Make	Buy and Leave Facilities Idle	Buy and Use Facilities for Other Products
Direct material	$30,000	-	-
Direct labor	30,000	-	-
Variable overhead	20,000	-	-
Fixed overhead	20,000	$11,000	$11,000
Purchase price from outsider	-	85,000	85,000
Total cost of obtaining brushes	$100,000	$96,000	$96,000
Profit contribution from other products	-	-	(6,000)
Net cost of obtaining 10,000 brushes	$100,000	$96,000	$90,000

Decision: The company should buy the brushes and use the facilities for other products.

Explanation:

The important point to remember is that relevant information differs among alternative courses of action. Continuing to make the brushes will cost the same $100,000 that it currently costs. The current cost to produce is relevant because it will change if the brushes are purchased. If the brushes are purchased, the relevant information is the purchase price and the amount of fixed overhead that will continue. The problem tells us that $9,000 of fixed overhead will be saved. Since total fixed overhead is $20,000, $11,000 ($20,000 - $9,000) of fixed overhead will continue, and the brushes will cost $96,000. If the facilities are used to earn an additional $6,000 profit, the net cost of the brushes is $90,000 ($96,000 - $6,000). For this alternative, the additional relevant information is the profit from the other product that could be produced.

CHAPTER 24 DEMONSTRATION PROBLEM 2 SOLVED AND EXPLAINED

Requirement 1

Unit costs for stuffed toys:

	Cost per Unit of Product		
	Total Variable Cost	Full Absorption Cost	Full Total Cost
Variable manufacturing cost	$2	$2	$2
Variable nonmanufacturing cost	1		1
Total variable cost	$3		
Fixed manufacturing cost		3[1]	3
Full absorption cost		$5	
Fixed nonmanufacturing cost			5[2]
Full total cost			$11

[1] Total fixed manufacturing costs / budgeted toys to be produced

= $1,650,000 / 550,000 = $3

[2] Total fixed nonmanufacturing costs / budgeted toys to be produced

= $2,750,000 / 550,000 = $5

Requirement 2

	Cost	Markup percentage to Achieve Desired Selling price of $19
Total variable	$3	($15 - $3) / $3 = 400 %
Full absorption	5	($15 - $5) / $5 = 200 %
Full total	11	($15 - $11) / $11 = 36.4 %

Requirement 3

(a) Total variable cost: Cost + markup

$3 + (400 % X $3) = $15

(b) Full absorption cost: Cost + markup

$5 + (200 % X $5) = $15

CHAPTER 25 DEMONSTRATION PROBLEM 1 SOLVED AND EXPLAINED

Requirement 1 (payback period)

$$\text{PAYBACK PERIOD} = \frac{\text{AMOUNT INVESTED}}{\text{EXPECTED ANNUAL NET CASH INFLOWS}}$$

$$= \frac{\$56{,}400}{\$14{,}100}$$

$$= 4 \text{ years}$$

Requirement 2 (accounting rate of return)

$$\text{AVERAGE AMOUNT INVESTED} = \frac{\text{AMOUNT INVESTED + RESIDUAL VALUE}}{2}$$

$$= \frac{\$56{,}400 + \$10{,}000}{2}$$

$$= \$33{,}200$$

$$\text{AVERAGE ANNUAL OPERATING INCOME FROM INVESTMENT} = \text{AVERAGE ANNUAL NET CASH INFLOW FROM OPERATIONS} - \text{ANNUAL DEPRECIATION}$$

$$= \$14{,}100 - [(\$56{,}400 - \$10{,}000) / 6]$$

$$= \$14{,}100 - \$7{,}733$$

$$= \$6{,}367$$

$$\text{ACCOUNTING RATE OF RETURN} = \frac{\text{AVERAGE ANNUAL OPERATING INCOME FROM INVESTMENT}}{\text{AVERAGE AMOUNT INVESTED}}$$

$$= \frac{\$6{,}367}{\$33{,}200}$$

$$= 19.2\ \%$$

Requirement 3 (net present value analysis)

	PV Factor		Net Cash Inflow		Present Value of Net Cash Inflow
Present value of annual net cash inflows	4.335	X	$14,100	=	$61,406
Present value of residual value	.564	X	$10,000	=	5,640
Present value of the machine					$67,045
Investment					(56,400)
Net present value of the machine					$10,645

Requirement 4 (decision)

Payback: Purchase the machine because the payback period (4 years) is less than the useful life (6 years).

Accounting rate of return: Purchase the machine because the return on the machine of 19.2 % exceeds the minimum desired rate of return (10 %).

Net present value: Purchase the machine because the net present value is positive.

Decision: Purchase the machine because it is recommended by all criteria.

CHAPTER 25 DEMONSTRATION PROBLEM 2 SOLVED AND EXPLAINED

Requirement 1

			Present Value Factor		PV of Cash Flows
Cash effects of operations:					
Pretax cash savings from operations	$600,000				
Income taxes at 40% on increased income	240,000				
After-tax effect on cash each year	$360,000	X	2.577	=	$927,720
Cash effects of depreciation deduction:					
Year / Deduction					
1 $700,000 X 40 %	$280,000	X	.926	=	648,200
2 $400,000 X 40 %	160,000	X	.857	=	137,120
3 $200,000 X 40 %	80,000	X	.794	=	63,500
Cash effects of disposal value:					
Sales price $100,000					
Book value -0-					
Net gain $100,000					
Income tax 40,000					
After-tax impact on cash	60,000	X	.794	=	47,640
Total After-tax effect in cash flows					$1,824,180
Investment					1,300,000
Net present value					$ 524,180

Requirement 2

			Present Value Factor		PV of Cash Flows
Cash effects of operations:					
Pretax cash savings from operations	$600,000				
Income taxes at 40% on increased income	240,000				
After-tax effect on cash each year	$360,000	X	2.577	=	$927,720
Cash effects of depreciation deduction:					
Year / Deduction					
1 $400,000 X 40 %	$160,000	X	.926	=	148,160
2 $400,000 X 40 %	160,000	X	.857	=	137,120
3 $400,000 X 40 %	160,000	X	.794	=	127,040

Cash effects of disposal value:				
Sales price	$100,000			
Book value	100,000			
Net gain	$ 0			
Income tax	0			
After-tax impact on cash		100,000 X .794	=	79,400
Total after-tax effect in cash flows				$1,419,440
Investment				1,300,000
Net present value				$ 119,440

The difference is a decrease of $404,740 ($524,180 - $119,440). Since the present value is still positive, the decision does not change.

CHAPTER 26 DEMONSTRATION PROBLEM 1 SOLVED AND EXPLAINED

Requirement 1

	Component External Sale	Consumer Internal Transfer	
Sales price	$ 60		$250
Variable costs:			
Assembly	45	$ 45	
CD Player	-	120	165
Contribution margin	$ 15		$ 85

Transfers should be made. The Consumer Division adds $190 ($250 - $60) to company revenue for each assembly transferred, but only $120 to variable cost. The company is $70 better off with the transfers.

Requirement 2

Without idle capacity, the market price will lead to the optimal decision. The Component Division will transfer assemblies to the Consumer Division because the Component Division receives the same price as it does for external sales. The Consumer Division will buy from the Component Division because the Consumer Division would have to pay the same price if it purchased assemblies from an outside supplier.

Requirement 3

Yes, the market price produces the optimal decision. The Consumer Division will continue to produce CD players, even though the cost of the assemblies is $60. Total variable costs are $180 ($60 for the assembly and $120 in the Consumer Division, resulting in a contribution margin of $70 ($250 - $180). The Consumer Products division will continue to produce CD players unless total variable costs exceeded the sales price, resulting in a negative contribution margin.

Requirement 4

The Component Division will set a minimum price equal to variable cost of $45. The Consumer Division will pay a maximum price of $60, which is the market price. The range is $45 to $60.

Requirement 5

Raising the transfer price from $60 to $90 will reduce U.S. income by $30 per unit and increase Hong Kong income by $30 per unit. The difference in tax rates is 15 percent (35 percent - 20 percent). $30 x 15 percent results in a tax savings of $4.50 per unit.

CHAPTER 26 DEMONSTRATION PROBLEM 2 SOLVED AND EXPLAINED

Requirement 1

Investment Turnover = Revenue ÷ Invested Capital

= (200,000 x \$6) ÷ \$750,000

= \$1,200,000 ÷ \$750,000

= 1.6

Profit Margin = Income ÷ Revenue

= [(200,000 x \$6) - (200,000 x \$4) - \$250,000] ÷ (200,000 x \$6)

= \$150,000 ÷ \$1,200,000

= .125 = 12.5 percent

ROI = Investment Turnover x Profit Margin

= 1.6 x 12.5 percent

= 20 percent

Requirement 2

Residual Income = Income - Imputed Interest on Capital

= \$150,000 - (\$750,000 x .12)

= \$150,000 - \$90,000

= \$60,000

Requirement 3

Existing ROI is 20 percent. The proposed project will yield ROI of 15 percent. Accepting a project that yields less than the current ROI will reduce current ROI. If evaluation is based on ROI and ROI is reduced by a new project, management will not want to accept the project.

Any project whose ROI is greater than the imputed interest rate (cost of capital in this problem) will increase residual income. The ROI of the proposed project is 15 percent, while the cost of capital is 12 percent. If evaluation is based on residual income, management will be inclined to accept the project.

<u>Requirement 4</u>

Increasing price to $6.50:

Investment Turnover = Revenue ÷ Invested Capital
= (200,000 x $6.50) ÷ $750,000
= $1,300,000 ÷ $750,000
= 1.733

Profit Margin = Income ÷ Revenue
= [(200,000 x $6.50) - (200,000 x $4) - $250,000] ÷ (200,000 x $6.50)
= $250,000 ÷ $1,200,000
= .20833 = 20.833 percent

ROI = Investment Turnover x Profit Margin
= 1.733 x 20.833 percent
= 36.1 percent

Reducing assets to $700,000:

Investment Turnover = Revenue ÷ Invested Capital
= (200,000 x $6) ÷ $700,000
= $1,200,000 ÷ $700,000
= 1.714

Profit Margin = Income ÷ Revenue
= [(200,000 x $6) - (200,000 x $4) - $250,000] ÷ (200,000 x $6)
= $150,000 ÷ $1,200,000
= .125 = 12.5 percent

ROI = Investment Turnover x Profit Margin
= 1.714 x 12.5 percent
= 21.4 percent

<u>Requirement 5</u> Raising prices increases both investment turnover and profit margin. Reducing invested capital increases investment turnover only. The price increase is more effective.

CHAPTER 27 DEMONSTRATION PROBLEM SOLVED AND EXPLAINED

1. Current Ratio = $\dfrac{\text{Current Assets}}{\text{Current Liabilities}}$

$$\frac{\$95{,}000 \text{ (current assets)}}{\$31{,}667 \text{ (current liabilities)}} = \frac{3}{1}$$

The current ratio is 3.

Current ratio is a frequently calculated liquidity ratio used to measure a firm's ability to pay current liabilities from current assets.

2. Acid-Test Ratio = $\dfrac{\text{Cash + Short-Term Investments + Net Current Receivables}}{\text{Current Liabilities}}$

$$\frac{\$13{,}300 \text{ (cash)} + \$8{,}200 \text{ (marketable securities)} + \$26{,}000 \text{ (receivables)}}{\$31{,}667 \text{ (current liabilities)}} = \frac{1.50}{1}$$

The acid-test ratio is 1.50.

This liquidity ratio measures a firm's ability to meet current liabilities from its most liquid assets. The acid-test ratio is often a more reliable indicator of solvency than the current ratio for firms with significant prepaid expenses and/or inventory because these current assets are less liquid than "quick assets."

3. Inventory Turnover = $\dfrac{\text{Cost of Goods Sold}}{\text{Average Inventory}}$ =

$$\frac{\$322{,}593 \text{ (cost of goods sold)}}{(\$45{,}000 + \$40{,}000) \div 2 \text{ (average inventory)}} = 7.59$$

The inventory turnover is 7.59 times a year.

This calculation aids in measuring a firm's ability to sell its inventory. Generally, firms seek a high turnover of inventory.

4. Days' Sales in Average Receivables = $\dfrac{\text{Average Net Accounts Receivable}}{\text{One Day's Sales}}$

One Day's Sales = $\dfrac{\text{Year's Sales}}{\text{365 Days}}$

$$\frac{(\$26{,}000 + \$24{,}000) \div 2 \text{ (average accounts receivable)}}{\$416{,}500 \div 365 \text{ days (daily sales)*}} = 21.9$$

* $416,500 ÷ 365 days = $1,141 (one day's sales)

There are 21.9 days of sales in the firm's average receivables.

Day's Sales and Accounts Receivable Turnover (in Requirement 5) both help to measure a firm's ability to collect its receivables. It would be necessary to know industry averages, past histories, and the firm's credit policy before commenting on what ratio the firm would consider acceptable.

5. Accounts Receivable Turnover = $\frac{\text{Net Credit Sales}}{\text{Average Net Receivables}}$

$$\frac{\$416{,}500 \text{ (net credit sales)}}{\$25{,}000 \text{ (average net receivables)}} = 16.7$$

The average account receivable "turned over" (or was collected) 16.7 times in 19X2.

6. Debt Ratio = $\frac{\text{Total Liabilities}}{\text{Total Assets}}$

$$\frac{\$31{,}667 + \$95{,}500 + \$1{,}100 + \$4{,}813 \text{ (total liabilities)}}{\$323{,}080 \text{ (total assets)}} = .41$$

Debt as a percentage of total assets is 41%.

The debt ratio indicates the proportion of asset acquisitions financed with debt instruments.

7. Times-Interest-Earned Ratio = $\frac{\text{Income from Operations}}{\text{Interest Expense}}$

$$\frac{\$52{,}688 \text{ (income from operations)}}{\$3{,}251 \text{ (interest expense)}} = 16.2$$

Interest expense was earned 16.2 times in 19X2.

Creditors prefer a relatively high number for this ratio because it measures a firm's ability to meet its interest obligations from operating income. Note that income from operations is earnings from operations, not net income.

8. Rate of Return on Net Sales = $\frac{\text{Net Income}}{\text{Net Sales}}$

$$\frac{\$42{,}000 \text{ (net income)}}{\$416{,}500 \text{ (net sales)}} = .101$$

The rate of return on net sales is 10.1%.

A measure of profitability, this calculation shows the percentage of each sales dollar that is ultimately earned as net income.

9. Rate of Return on Total Assets = $\frac{\text{Net Income + Interest Expense}}{\text{Average Total Assets}}$

$$\frac{\$42{,}000 \text{ (net income)} + \$3{,}251 \text{ (interest expense)}}{(\$323{,}080 + \$330{,}900) \div 2 \text{ (average assets)}} = .138$$

<u>The rate of return earned on total assets for 19X2 was 13.8%</u>.

This calculation is useful in gauging the profitability of assets used in the business. Interest expense is added to net income in order to reduce distortions from the rate of returns that would be caused by the financing cost itself.

10. Rate of Return on Common Stockholders' Equity = $\frac{\text{Net Income - Preferred Dividends}}{\text{Average Common Stockholders' Equity}}$

$$\frac{\$42{,}000 \text{ (net income)}}{(\$190{,}000 + \$197{,}000) \div 2} = .217$$

<u>The 19X2 rate of return on common stockholders' equity was 21.7%</u>.

This calculation measures the profitability of assets financed by the common stockholders' investment. Common stockholders would be elated with a return of close to 22%.

11. Price/Earnings Ratio = $\frac{\text{Market Price Per Share of Common Stock}}{\text{Earnings Per Share}}$

$$\frac{\$8 \text{ (market price per share)}}{\$.40 \text{ (earnings per share)*}} = \frac{20}{1}$$

* $42,000 ÷ 105,000 avg. outstanding shares of common stock = EPS of $.40.

<u>The P/E ratio is 20</u>, a benchmark that relates the market price to the earnings of a single share of common stock.

12. Book Value Per Share of Common Stock = $\frac{\text{Total Stockholders' Equity - Preferred Equity}}{\text{Number of Shares of Common Stock Outstanding}}$

$$\frac{\$190{,}000 \text{ (total common stockholders' equity)}}{110{,}000 \text{ (shares outstanding at year end)}} = \$1.73 \text{ per share}$$

<u>The common stock book value per share is $1.73</u>.

The <u>recorded value</u> (as opposed to the market value) of each share of stock is its <u>book</u> value.

13. $$\text{Dividend Yield} = \frac{\text{Dividend per Share of Common Stock}}{\text{Market Price per Share of Common Stock}}$$

$$\frac{\$.60}{\$8 \text{ (market price)}} = .075$$

The dividend yield for 19X2 is 7.5%

The dividend yield measures the percentage of the stock's market value that is returned annually to the owners as dividends.

Points to Remember

The preparation of financial statements is only the initial stage in the analysis of a firm's performance. While a review of these statements provides a great deal of information, more thorough analysis requires that the information be interpreted in light of current economic conditions. In addition, financial statement analysis should highlight trends within the firm itself and trends within the industry among competitors in the same line of business. There are three principal means of accomplishing this: horizontal analysis, vertical analysis, and use of financial ratios.

1. **Horizontal analysis** shows percentage change in individual financial statement items over time. Increases (or decreases) in sales, cost of sales, administrative costs, and net income have more meaning when the changes are reviewed in conjunction with the firm's performance over time. In fact, most published annual reports include the complete preceding year as well as a five-year summary of prior years.

2. **Vertical analysis** is an essential tool of analysis when quantifying performance within a given industry because firms differ greatly in size. By converting each figure in the income statement and balance sheet to a percentage of another (typically a percentage of net sales), more meaning can be "carved out" of the information for use by the wide variety of financial statement users.

3. **Financial ratios** are mathematical formulas that quantify the relationship between two or more items reported in the financial statements. Ratios are used to assess and compare a firm's liquidity, profitability, rate of return, and ability to meet debt obligations.

Note: One of the most common mistakes students make is forgetting to use the average amount of inventory, accounts receivable, or shares outstanding in some of the formulas. It is important that an average be used to reduce distortions that might occur if only year-end balances were used.